This book is dedicated to all born again Christians, that they might know that the Bible has the utmost Truth and Authority.

ISBN: 978-981-11-2467-9
© 2018 by Samuel Ken En Gan
Published by APD SKEG Pte Ltd
All rights reserved. No part of this book may be reproduced without prior permission of the author or proper acknowledgements

Cover designs are © 2018 by Samuel Gan
Front cover picture shows the Judean desert near Timnah taken in December 2014.
Dissemination by email or printing with respect to authorship is encouraged.

Author's Note and Acknowledgements

This book is an accumulated effort of simple research to further the understanding of the teachings of the Holy Bible using a psychological perspective. "All roads lead to Rome", and it is my belief that all academic fields that seek truth, will find it when correctly illuminated and within the framework of the Scriptures, that is, the Truth of God. This is thus my attempt to re-look at many aspects of psychology, under the authority of Word of God, and to investigate the psychological impact of the Word of God on our personal daily lives. The writings are made suitable for the non-academic reader, so one need not necessarily be a psychologist to appreciate all the points.

As with all good psychological reports, introspective analysis is required, thus I must state that my premise stems from my belief that the Word of God is inspired and preserved perfectly in the Masoretic Text and Textus Receptus, thereby, the utmost absolute authority over all things. While God has allowed man the ability to think, ponder and analyze, which are attributes that spawned the academic disciplines that exist today, there is a need to realign with God's Word. Harnessed in the right manner under the guidance of the Scriptures, believers need not reject nor fear apparent contradictions to God's Word within the pursuit of these disciplines, for God's Word will always emerge victorious to be the sole objective, unmovable, and steadfast Truth.

Why is this book an E-book?

As with my previous Christian books, in order not to compromise unnecessarily, and to have the materials freely accessible to all; regardless of geographical location, marketing limitations, and cost restrictions, the solution was to release this work as a standalone E-book. If the content glorifies the Lord in the way He is pleased, then let the book be used and be disseminated widely. If there be heresy or compromise, then let the E-book fade into obscurity as it would deserve.

I have little doubt that this book would be severely attacked by secular psychologists and even some Christians. If there be any unbiblical basis, I gladly recant. If there be none, He is my shield. Nonetheless, I confess that any good from this book is of the Lord's, and any fault is mine and mine alone. However, it is my aim to not compromise biblical principles in the interpretation and I mention upfront that all interpretations would be biased to my understanding of biblical principles and truths.

Acknowledgements

Finally, as with any such piece of work, a lot of effort and support was offered by family and friends. While my heartfelt thanks are extended to everyone, I reserve my greatest gratitude to the Lord.

Availability

This E-book can be obtained directly from the author by email at absolutely no charge. One site to download the latest edition is

https://tinyurl.com/apsychguide

Other books:

"A Practical Guide to the Logic, Philosophy, and Thoughts of Christianity" (1st Edition 2009, 2nd Edition 2014, 3rd Edition 2016 ISBN: 978-981-09-8412-0) - http://tinyurl.com/apracguidechrist
http://www.wattpad.com/2553841-a-practical-guide-to-the-logic-philosophy-and
Wattpad code : 2553841

"Another Practical Guide to the Logic, Philosophy, and Thoughts of Christianity" (1st Edition 2012; 2nd Edition 2014, 3rd Edition 2016, ISBN: 978-981-09-8414-4) - http://tinyurl.com/anotherpracguidechrist
http://www.wattpad.com/2560218-another-practical-guide-to-the-logic-philosophy#
Wattpad code : 2560218

A related book "A Guide to the Biblical Lands: Jordan and Israel" (2nd Edition 2016 ISBN: 9789810984151) can be obtained at http://tinyurl.com/biblelandsguide

"The Interplanetary Visit – Mission: Milky Way" (1st Edition, 2005; Revised Edition 2017, ISBN: 1-4137-6021-X) - http://tinyurl.com/IPVMMW2017

God bless,

Samuel Gan

Jupitian2000@hotmail.com

August 2018.

Table of Contents

Psychology based articles that affirm the Authority of God's Word   6

Article 1: The role for Psychology in Christian Theology   7

Article 2: Psychology of Music sheds light on David's music to King Saul.   12

Appendix A: The relaxation effects of stimulative and sedative music on mathematics anxiety: A perception to physiology model   15

Article 3: Self-Analysis in the 16th century Reformation   27

Article 4: A testimony of what the various disciplines led a sinner to see the Truth of the Bible.   31

Article 5: Stockholm syndrome and the election of God   33

Article 6: Psychological tests and Intelligent Design   36

Article 7: Problems of Charismatic Christianity   39

Article 8: Speaking/Teaching Animals in the Bible   46

Article 9: Loose Language   48

Article 10: Demonology   50

Article 11: Singlehood, Marriage, Friendships   55

Article 12: Importance of Words - Part 1: Repent   59

Article 13: Importance of Words - Part 2: Heart speak   61

Article 14: "Into the Woods"   63

Psychology based articles that affirm the Authority of God's Word

Article 1 – The role for Psychology in Christian Theology

Psychology is a field that very much deserves more credit when it comes to being recognized as an academic field to search for the truth. By the proponents of the hard sciences (physics, chemistry, biology, etc.), psychology is regarded as a soft science, capable only of making associations and correlations. In the church, it is even more misunderstood. Some churches rely on it too much, such that they do not rely on the power of the gospel, while the opposite camp regards it as some form of demonic/mystic arts, particularly when dealing with hypnosis and charisma.

Even in the circle of science-based creation apologetics, Psychology is not given its due credit as it is deemed to be too associative, often without clear cause and effect and "not firm" in its findings to be suitable for apologetic use. Yet, let us never rely on non-biblical findings for our foundation, even if it were the hard sciences. For nothing but the Word of God will fade away.

Matthew 24:35 - Heaven and earth shall pass away, but my words shall not pass away.

Nonetheless, psychology does reveals a lot in creation apologetics. Let us remember from the Scriptures:

2 Corinthians 10:15 – Casting down imaginations, and every high thing that exalteth itself against the knowledge of God, and bringing into captivity every thought to the obedience of Christ;

that we have a Christian duty to take captive the data and theories of psychology and bring it to the obedience of Christ.

What has psychology shown us?

Of all the sciences, it is the only one that can effectively show us the horrible state of the Fall recorded in Genesis. No hard sciences can address the topic of Evil. In my own research, Psychology is the only scientific field that has and can study the fallen mind. Every psychology student would have undoubtedly studied Philip Zimbardo's Stanford Prison Experiment (https://en.wikipedia.org/wiki/Stanford_prison_experiment and http://www.prisonexp.org/conclusion) that revealed the wickedness in the hearts of man in this famous role-playing exercise that quickly took a downward spiral towards amorality and evil. Although the original experiment was performed in August 1971, the findings were relooked again to explain the Abu Ghraib prison treatment by the American soldiers in 2003 (https://en.wikipedia.org/wiki/Abu_Ghraib_torture_and_prisoner_abuse).

A quick background to the famous Stanford Prison experiment is that Professor Zimbardo, a professor in psychology in Stanford University recruited college students randomly assigned to be either guards or prisoners in a make-pretend prison within the university. Although the experiment was meant to last for two weeks, it was halted in just six days when the students embraced their roles too far to the extent of melting out or accepting psychological torture. Zimbardo interpreted this as the corruptible nature of man when given power, something he later called "The Lucifer Effect" when taking into accounting Milgram's psychology studies.

Stanley Milgram, a Yale University psychology has many experiments on obedience which would also without a doubt be covered in basic psychology courses. Milgram found that most people were willing to administer shocks up to 450 Volts when under instruction to teach. These experiments were conferred the classification of "Psychology of Evil", a more formal name than the "Lucifer effect" by Philip Zimbardo.

Interestingly, neither Zimbardo nor Milgram were professing Christians, and yet, they found evidence for Evil. There are to date, many more modern versions of these psychology experiments, and there is a ton of other evidences for the evil in mankind. To name just another, is the bystander effect" or "Genovese syndrome" in psychology, after the Kitty Genovese murder case (https://en.wikipedia.org/wiki/Murder_of_Kitty_Genovese) where a lady, stabbed, raped, and stabbed again over a period of time, was not aided by anyone despite having several witnesses having noticed or heard the cries for help.

Even psychologists cannot help but wonder that if evil exists in the hearts of men, where did it come from? If there is evil, there has to be good. How did evil come in? These are questions that atheists - psychologists or not -cannot answer. For if there is good and evil, a series of logical deductions would point to a Judge above good and evil to define them in the first place. And this conscious, discerning Judge is undoubtedly God in the final stage of logical reasoning.

This is great apologetic material, for evil is for once, proven in an academic discipline, by psychology. If there is no evil, there is no suitable explanation for the horrid behavior of man. Why would man evolve such systematic evilness? It certainly did not just happen, chance or not. In fact, on the origins of evil, there has been no agreed consensus by atheistic psychologists.

To the Bible believing Christian, the psychological evidence of Evil is clear evidence for the Calvinistic view of Man's fallen state - man is totally depraved, and incapable of doing good. In fact, even when I was a psychology student, I found innumerable evidence in my social psychology modules on top of the cases already mentioned. Today, psychoanalysis and everything Freudian is dismissed by many psychologists, however they are methods that can reveal the wickedness of man e.g. the application of introspection and other self-analyses will most certainly reveal that almost all our motives and desires are borne out of the wickedness of the heart. As aptly put, Jeremiah 17:9 – "The heart *is* deceitful above all *things*, and desperately wicked: who can know it?" Self-analysis alone may not be sufficient, for it is the light of God's law that shows us our wickedness. Under the illumination of the Scriptures, psychoanalytic methods certainly reveal the dark inner workings of the mind. Yet, without the illumination of the Scriptures, even brilliant but godless psychologists cannot make the connection between Scriptural truths and psychological findings, the latter would only make sense when taking into account of the Fall in Genesis. Thus, the Bible remains the ultimate authority and unifying guide, not only for explanation, but for all things.

The problem comes when without the guide of the Bible, the interpretations become wayward and even self-contradicting, thus there is often confusion or controversy in psychology itself. This is evident also for psychological studies on sexual behavior, especially those from the infamous Kinsey Institute (which is most known for findings on infidelity and deviant sexual behavior of the average American to be rampant). Just because something is commonly performed by most people, does not make it acceptable. Rather, such debauchery is clearly the evidence of the total depravity of man.

There is no lack of data from psychological studies that affirm the fallen state of man. Some examples mentioned in passing include how many times we lie and how selfish desires are present in all human relationships. Psychology does a great deal to investigate these things that the "hard sciences" cannot. And these are great apologetic material. The discerning Christian should certainly reject the unbiblical practices and interpretations. but not the data or observation, which neither has will nor desire to prove or disprove the Bible. Guided by the authority of the Scriptures, all knowledge can be tied together, and they are all in harmony in obedience to the knowledge of Christ.

Let us not throw out the baby with the bath water as Peter almost did for the Gentiles in Acts 10:9-16. All wisdom and knowledge are of the Lord. It is man who had perverted all things good in the Fall. Under the guidance and authority of the Word of God, they will make sense and give glory to God.

As it is with psychology, it is with all knowledge.

Article 2 – Psychology of Music sheds light on David's music to King Saul.

1 Samuel 16:14-23

But the Spirit of the LORD departed from Saul, and an evil spirit from the LORD troubled him. And Saul's servants said unto him, Behold now, an evil spirit from God troubleth thee. Let our lord now command thy servants, which are before thee, to seek out a man, who is a cunning player on an harp: and it shall come to pass, when the evil spirit from God is upon thee, that he shall play with his hand, and thou shalt be well.

And Saul said unto his servants, Provide me now a man that can play well, and bring him to me. Then answered one of the servants, and said, Behold, I have seen a son of Jesse the Bethlehemite, that is cunning in playing, and a mighty valiant man, and a man of war, and prudent in matters, and a comely person, and the LORD is with him. Wherefore Saul sent messengers unto Jesse, and said, Send me David thy son, which is with the sheep. And Jesse took an ass laden with bread, and a bottle of wine, and a kid, and sent them by David his son unto Saul. And David came to Saul, and stood before him: and he loved him greatly; and he became his armourbearer. And Saul sent to Jesse, saying, Let David, I pray thee, stand before me; for he hath found favour in my sight. And it came to pass, when the evil spirit from God was upon Saul, that David took an harp, and played with his hand: so Saul was refreshed, and was well, and the evil spirit departed from him.

The effect of music in the account recorded in 1 Samuel 16:14-23 is not one of folklore perception of evil spirits causing migraines, but is a supernatural deed performed in the permissive and decretive will of God. In this account, psychological studies can shed some light here.

Based on a psychological study performed by my research team on the "P2P model" (see Appendix A), David is most likely to play the harp for Saul for at least thirty minutes before the soothing physiological effects are fully effected on Saul. Such understanding thus provides an insight to how Saul could recover, and yet still have time plot to kill David by later throwing a spear as recorded in 1 Samuel 18:11 and 19:10.

It is in no short matter of seconds that Saul felt better, nor was it under the influence of the evil spirit that Saul plotted to kill David. It was from none other than the jealousy of his own heart. Saul bore the responsibility alone. And it was very likely some time into David's music before Saul could recover his sanity sufficiently to plot and act out the evilness of his heart.

To provide some basic background to the psychology study, anxiety was induced in human volunteers through math questions (mathematics anxiety). The anxiety was measured via their state anxiety questionnaires (for the current state of anxiety) and physiological parameters (blood pressure, heart rate). It was found that exposure to calming music (less than 60 beats per minute) can reduce the anxiety whereas fast-paced music did not.

If Saul was tormented by the evil spirit to be psychologically anxious and restless, David's music would very likely be sedative (slow tempo or beat) as psalms and hymns would be. This makes sense as the harp is not an instrument for fast rapid music (it would be difficult to play 'Flight of the Bumblebee' on a harp). And so the account is not without scientific and physiological basis. It should be noted that the spiritual and scientific aspects of this account are not mutually exclusive, but rather both harmoniously affirm the account.

This affirms the authority of the Bible being supreme authority on all spiritual and also scientific matters. And the subservient sciences, when guided by the Holy Ghost, can shed light in our understanding of the account as well.

Appendix A:

Article

The relaxation effects of stimulative and sedative music on mathematics anxiety: A perception to physiology model

Psychology of Music
2016, Vol. 44(4) 730–741
© The Author(s) 2015
Reprints and permissions:
sagepub.co.uk/journalsPermissions.nav
DOI: 10.1177/0305735615590430
pom.sagepub.com
$SAGE

Samuel Ken-En Gan, Keane Ming-Jie Lim and Yu-Xuan Haw

Abstract
Previous research on music and mathematics anxiety has relied primarily on self-reports without biological measurements. To address whether these parameters were correlated, we included blood pressure physiological measures, the State-Trait Anxiety Inventory (STAI) and the Mathematics Anxiety Rating Scale (MARS) in our study. One hundred and five psychology undergraduates were assigned to sedative, stimulative and "no music" conditions while completing Cambridge GCE O Level mathematical questions. Anxiety was measured pre-, during and posttest. Results showed that MARS was positively correlated with STAI, but not with the physiological measures. A 3 × 3 mixed ANOVA showed differences between the sedative and no music condition for the measures of STAI and MARS, but not for the physiological measures. Further analyses using t-tests found sedative music to elicit a pronounced decrease in systolic blood pressure and the stimulative music to have minimal effect. To explain these findings and the discrepancy with previous studies, we propose a Perception-to-Physiology model for the effect of music in anxiety.

Keywords
mathematics anxiety, music, physiological, relaxation, self-reports

Mathematics anxiety is a specific form of state anxiety proposed to cause poor mathematical performance (Ashcraft, 2002; Cemen, 1987). It elicits physiological responses similar to that of generalized anxiety (Mattarella-Micke, Mateo, Kozak, Foster, & Beilock, 2011; Sheffield & Hunt,

---

James Cook University, Singapore
Bioinformatics Institute, Agency for Science, Technology, and Research (A*STAR), Singapore
p53 Laboratory, Agency for Science, Technology, and Research (A*STAR), Singapore

Corresponding author:
Samuel Gan, Bioinformatics Institute, A*STAR, 30 Biopolis Street, #07-01, Matrix 138671, Singapore.
Email: samuelg@bii.a-star.edu.sg

2006), and is a learned response arising from prior negative learning experiences and poor performances (Cemen, 1987). Mathematics anxiety maybe comparable to preoperative-induced anxiety in the consequences caused, and is prevalent in the student population (Jones, 2001). It affects students majoring in arts, mathematics, psychology and engineering subjects (Sheffield & Hunt, 2006) by eliciting fear of math problems and negatively affecting their working memory (Ashcraft & Kirk, 2001).

To alleviate general anxiety, music was found to be a useful tool (Nilsson, 2008; Pelletier, 2004) in promoting physiological relaxation (heart rate and blood pressure), particularly sedative music, which is characterized by slow tempo of 60 to 80 beats per minute (bpm) with a soft dynamic range (Gadberry, 2011). On the contrary, stimulative music (characterized by fast tempo and broad dynamic range; see Hooper, 2012) arouses the listener and elicits a feeling of excitement (Lingham & Theorell, 2009). This property of music can be explained by the entrainment phenomenon—where two separate rhythms synchronize into a common phase (Clayton, Sager, & Will, 2005) — and has been used to calm the following: preoperative patients (Hamel, 2001), Stroop experiment participants (Walworth, 2003), videotaped oral presenters (Knight & Rickard, 2001), test subjects performing a mental rotation task (Burns et al., 2002), those performing mental arithmetic tasks (Chafin, Roy, Gerin, & Christenfeld, 2004), and students taking an algebra exam (Hardie, 1990).

Specific to mathematics anxiety, music was potent enough to reduce anxiety with a short 10 minute pre-exam exposure (Haynes, 2004). However, much of the research (Burns, et al., 2002; Gadberry, 2011; Haynes, 2004) is based on self-reported measures (i.e. perceived anxiety) which are confounded by self-biases (McCroskey, 1997), and have neither included physiological measures nor found significant correlation between self-reported and physiological measures commonly used for studies on anxiety and stress (Burns, Labbe, Williams, & McCall, 1999; Burns, et al., 2002; Labbe, Schmidt, Babin, & Pharr, 2007). This is shown in a study of preoperative patients, where differences in state anxiety but not in physiological blood pressure measurements were found (Lee, Henderson, and Shum, 2004). Nonetheless, Labbe et al. (2007) were able to find reduction in both self-reports and physiological anxiety measurements for mathematical anxiety after 20 minutes of exposure to sedative music, suggesting that the differences in musical exposure times accounted for the varying physiological effects (Lee et al., 2004).

To address the differences in the physiological effect of music on anxiety, we utilized both self-reports and physiological anxiety measures in our study. We have chosen to use mathematics anxiety in our study since literature on this area is limited, and it is a safe form of inducible anxiety that can be validated with STAI and MARS.

The hypotheses of the present study are as listed:

1: STAI and MARS would be positively correlated.
1A: STAI and physiological measurements (heart rate, systolic and diastolic blood pressure) would be positively correlated.
1B: MARS and the physiological measurements would be positively correlated.
2: Sedative music would be perceived to be more relaxing than stimulative music.
2A: Sedative music would reduce physiological arousal (heart rate, systolic and diastolic blood pressure) in a more pronounced manner than the stimulative music.

Method

Participants

A total of 105 psychology undergraduate students were recruited from James Cook University, Singapore. Participants consisted of 63% females ($n = 66$) and 37% males ($n = 39$) aged from

19 to 31 years old ($M = 22.23$, $SD = 2.08$). To standardize prior mathematical experiences and abilities and minimize influences on mathematical anxiety (Cemen, 1987), all participants recruited were Singapore citizens who studied up to tertiary levels in the country. A total of 70 participants received course credits for their respective psychology courses, while the remaining 35 participants were volunteers.

Materials

Self-reported measures. The state portion (Form X-1) of the STAI (Spielberger, Gorsuch, & Lushene, 1970) was used to measure the self-reported state anxiety levels. This 20-item instrument required participants to rate their current anxiety state on a four-point Likert scale from 1 (*not at all*) to 4 (*very much so*). The measure consisted of 10 positively (e.g., 'I feel calm') and negatively (e.g., 'I feel anxious') phrased items. The test–retest reliability ranged from .16 to .54 from the test norm in previous research (Spielberger et al., 1970) due to the situational changes at the point of administration. The STAI had a Cronbach alpha ranging from .83 to .92 (Spielberger et al., 1970), supported by studies on a college sample (Fonseca-Pedrero, Paino, Sierra-Baigrie, Lemos-Giraldez, & Muniz, 2012) and Asian participants (Hishinuma et al., 2000). In the current study, a similar high Cronbach alpha ranging between .86 and .90 was found.

The abbreviated version of the MARS (Alexander & Martray, 1989) was used to measure the extent of mathematics anxiety. This 25-item inventory required participants to rate their anxiety in each scenario in the statements (e.g., 'being given a set of multiplication problems to solve') on a five-point Likert scale from 1 (*not at all*) to 5 (*very much*). The total possible scores ranged from 25 to 125 with higher scores indicating greater mathematics anxiety. The MARS is widely used due to its validity and reliability (Plake & Parker, 1982). It has a two week test–retest reliability of .86 (Alexander & Martray, 1989) and an internal consistency with Cronbach alpha of .95 (Baloglu & Kocak, 2006). Similarly, the present study showed a high internal consistency with Cronbach alpha range between .95 and .97.

Numbers were assigned to the two self-reported measures (e.g., 'Questionnaire 1') to prevent identification of the measures. Upon the completion of both self-reported measures, participants continued on the remaining mathematical questions. To reduce experimental errors, the two halves of the task were counterbalanced across participants.

Physiological measures. The physiological measures of anxiety were assessed using an automated blood pressure monitor (Omron HEM 7200). The arm cuff was placed on the non-dominant arm to measure heart rate, systolic and diastolic blood pressure as according to the manufacturer's instructions.

Mathematical task and post-task questionnaire. The mathematical task consisted of 12 questions, taken from the compilation of past University of Cambridge GCE O Level advanced and elementary mathematics examinations (Yun, 2013a, 2013b). GCE O Level exams are typically taken at the end of secondary school education at the age of 16 years. The post-task questionnaire consisted of three sections (see supplementary materials). The first part consisted of demographic questions, while the second part required the participants to rate their interest in the solutions to the mathematical task on a five-point Likert scale from 1 (*not at all*) to 5 (*very much*). The third part of the questionnaire was only completed by participants in the musical conditions, and consisted of questions regarding their preference and familiarity regarding the music played (e.g., 'how familiar are you with the music you just listened to?' on a scale of 1 to 5).

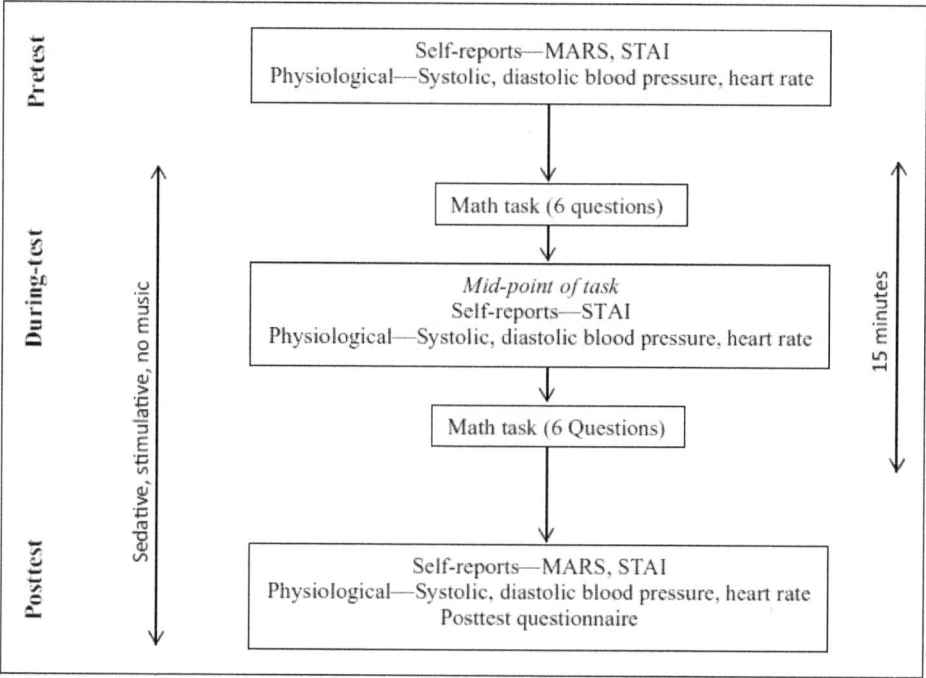

Figure 1. Flowchart of experiment procedure.

Music. Two pieces of music were used in the study. The sedative piece of music was Beethoven's Moonlight Sonata No.14 in C-sharp Minor Op. 72 No. 2, and the stimulative music used was Camille Saints-Saens' Allegro Moderato, Symphony No. 3 Op. 78, third movement. These two pieces of music were selected because the bpm were within the characteristics of sedative and stimulative music (see "Introduction" above, and Dove, 2009; Hooper, 2012). The music was played through a set of headphones (Audio-Technica ATH-T200 dynamic headphones) at a fixed volume of 7 on a Windows Vista computer.

Procedure

The design of this study was a pretest-posttest design (see Figure 1). Self-reported anxiety and physiological measures were performed pre-, during- and post-math task in order to capture the rise, peak, and decrease of anxiety levels. The participants were seated in a cubicle within the research laboratory and were given the consent form and information sheet prior to the start of the experiment.

Pretest. Upon consent, the arm cuff for the blood pressure monitor was fitted on the participant's non-dominant arm. The participants were asked to sit quietly for 5 minutes for baseline measurements before they worked on the MARS and STAI. While completing these inventories, participants' blood pressure and heart rate readings were measured. The mean of three readings, recorded at 1 minute intervals was calculated (measure adapted from the procedures as previously performed in Gan, Loh, & Seet, 2003; Yew, Lim, Haw, & Gan, 2015).

During the test. Participants were allocated to one of the musical conditions (sedative, stimulative, no music), which was played from the start of the mathematical task till the debriefing session. Prior to starting the mathematical task, the participants were informed of the countdown for each question at the bottom right corner of the computer screen, added deliberately to increase time-awareness pressure (DeDonno & Demaree, 2008). A total of 12 questions were presented as a timed PowerPoint slideshow, and participants had between 30 seconds to 1 minute per question, depending on the difficulty of the question. No calculators were allowed, and the participants' performances were scored according to the intermediate workings by the same researcher. At the mid-point (after six questions), the participants completed the 'during-test' STAI, and had their blood pressure and heart rate readings taken in two consecutive readings.

Posttest. Upon completion of the mathematical task (total of 12 questions), participants were asked to complete the 'posttest' STAI and MARS while having their final blood pressure parameters measured (similar to the procedure in the pretest phase). After debrief, the participants were thanked for their participation. The entire experiment took less than 30 minutes.

Ethical considerations

Ethical approval (H5139) was given by James Cook University Human Research Ethics Committee. The experiment was deemed a low-risk study.

Results

The data were analyzed using the IBM Statistical Package for Social Science (SPSS) version 20.0. All tests conducted were two-tailed with an alpha value of .05 unless otherwise stated. Table 1 shows the means and standard deviations for the physiological and self-reported measures of mathematics anxiety by experimental conditions.

Baseline measures

A series of one-way between-groups analysis of variance (ANOVA) were conducted to assess the differences in the baseline measures. There were no significant differences between the conditions (sedative, stimulative, no music) on the baseline measurements of STAI, heart rate, systolic and diastolic blood pressure (all with $p > 0.05$).

Efficacy of mathematical task

The efficacy of the mathematical task in inducing mathematics anxiety was assessed by comparing the pre and post MARS scores of participants in the control (no music) condition. A paired-samples t-test showed that there was a significant increase in MARS scores from pre-test to post-test (Table 1), $t(34) = 6.35$, $p < .001$. The mean increase in MARS scores was 15.00 with CI [10.20, 19.80] and $\eta^2 = .54$.

Hypothesis 1—correlation between physiological and self-reported measures

To examine the relationship between the physiological (heart rate, systolic and diastolic blood pressure) and self-reported measurements (STAI and MARS), bivariate Pearson product-moment correlation using the mean score of each variable at pre- and posttest was performed. Table 2 shows a positive correlation between the STAI and MARS at pretest and posttest, but a

Table 1. Means and standard deviations of variables by experimental conditions.

Variables	Sedative (n = 35)		Stimulative (n = 35)		Control (n = 35)	
	M	SD	M	SD	M	SD
STAI (State)						
Pre	38.80	7.46	38.09	8.17	36.17	6.01
During	46.97	8.85	50.51	9.56	52.00	7.87
Post	44.51	9.27	49.46	10.04	50.00	8.73
MARS						
Pre	68.43	16.35	61.49	15.71	63.17	18.76
Post	74.49	19.31	72.49	20.76	78.17	22.38
Systolic BP (mmHg)						
Pre	111.61	11.50	112.50	11.66	110.70	10.19
During	107.44	10.27	110.73	11.66	109.01	9.31
Post	105.57	9.15	109.13	10.21	107.20	10.17
Diastolic BP (mmHg)						
Pre	69.71	8.14	69.16	6.13	70.04	8.06
During	67.64	7.91	68.54	7.16	67.26	8.87
Post	67.18	6.51	68.25	6.99	68.53	8.32
Heart rate (bpm)						
Pre	78.83	9.13	80.19	14.39	76.39	11.44
During	77.89	9.12	79.80	12.67	77.11	11.13
Post	79.64	8.62	81.06	13.36	77.85	11.45

Note: Pre = pretest; During = midpoint of mathematical task; Post = posttest; BP = blood pressure.

Table 2. Pearson's correlation between physiological and self-reported measures. (a) Pretest.

Measure	STAI	MARS	SysBP	DiasBP	H/R
STAI	–	.370**	.041	.137	.188
MARS		–	–.220*	–.133	.150

2b. Posttest.

Measure	STAI	MARS	SysBP	DiasBP	H/R
STAI	–	.524**	–.068	.123	.133
MARS		–	–.325**	–.137	.089

Note: SysBP = systolic blood pressure; DiasBP = diastolic blood pressure; H/R = Heart rate. *$p < .05$. **$p < .01$.

negative correlation between MARS and the systolic blood pressure. There was no significant correlation found between STAI and the rest of the physiological measures.

Hypothesis 2—effect of music on mathematics anxiety

The effect of the experimental conditions (sedative, stimulative, no music) on mathematics anxiety was investigated using the reactivity measure (the difference in the measures between each time period, i.e., during-pre, post-during, post-pre). A series of 3 (sedative, stimulative, and

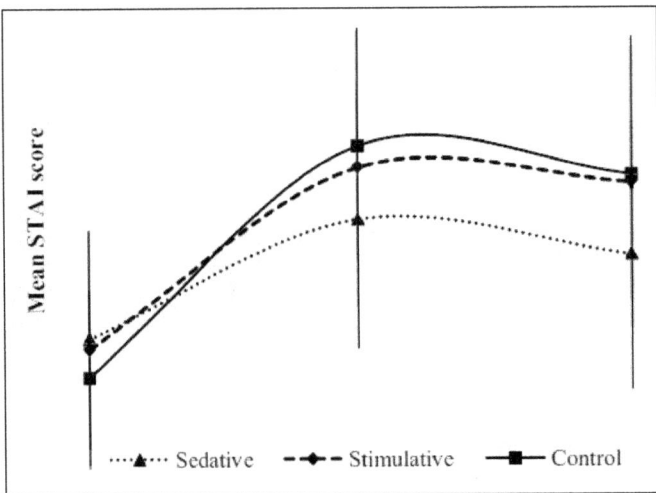

Figure 2. Mean STAI score between time period and experimental condition. The error bars represent standard deviation.

no music) × 3 (during-pre, post-during, post-pre) mixed ANOVAs were conducted on each of the measures (STAI, systolic and diastolic blood pressure, and heart rate). The between-subjects variable was the musical condition, while the within subjects variable was time period. The assumption of homogeneity of variance (tested using Levene's test of equality of error variances as well as test of normality) was met. However, the Mauchly's test of sphericity was violated, hence a Greenhouse-Geisser correction was applied to the degrees of freedom. All reported effects were partial η^2, with a one-tailed alpha value.

For STAI, there was a significant main effect found for: (1) music, $F(2, 102) = 8.12, p < .001, \eta^2 = .137$; (2) time, $F(1.279, 130.476) = 169.42, p < .001, \eta^2 = .624$; and (3) an interaction effect between the experimental conditions and the time period, $F(2.558, 130.476) = 4.63, p = .003, \eta^2 = .083$. Post-hoc comparison using Tukey HSD (honest significant difference) test showed the mean change scores of STAI (see Figure 2) for the sedative condition ($M = 3.81$) to be significantly different from the stimulative ($M = 7.58$) and no music condition ($M = 9.22$). There was no significant difference between the stimulative and no music condition.

For physiological measures, there was a significant main effect of time for (1) systolic blood pressure (see Figure 3), $F(1.337, 136.339) = 9.26, p < .001, \eta^2 = .083$; (2) diastolic blood pressure, $F(1.159, 118.253) = 6.05, p = .006, \eta^2 = .056$; and (3) heart rate, $F(1.256, 128.062) = 4.16, p = .017, \eta^2 = .039$. There was no significant main effect of the musical conditions on systolic and diastolic blood pressure, and heart rate (all with $p > 0.05$). No statistical significance was found for the interaction between time and musical conditions on systolic and diastolic blood pressure, and heart rate.

To further investigate the significant effect of time observed on the variables (STAI, systolic and diastolic blood pressure, and heart rate), paired-samples t-tests were conducted to compare the differences between each time period (during-pre, post-during, post-pre) within each musical condition (see Table 3). Significant differences were found between STAI and systolic blood pressure at the post-pre time period (all $p < .001$) for all musical conditions. Furthermore, the rate of decrease for the sedative condition was twice that of stimulative and control. Significant differences for diastolic blood pressure were found at the post-pre time period (all $p < .05$) for both the sedative and control conditions. There were no significant differences for heart rate

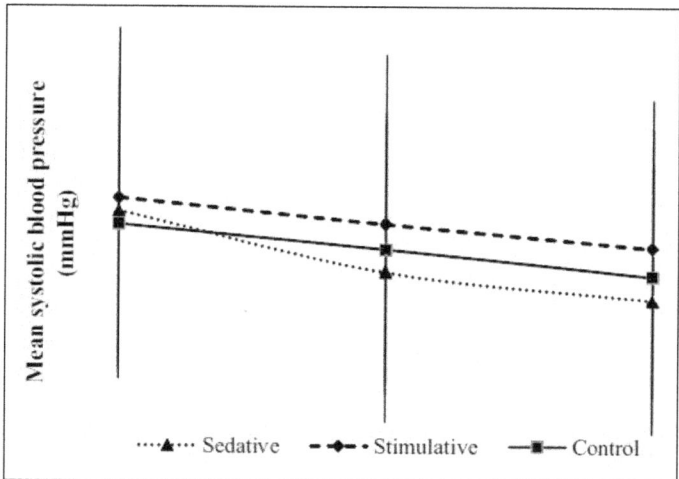

Figure 3. Mean systolic blood pressure between time period and experimental condition. The error bars represent standard deviation.

Table 3. Summary of changed scores for variables by musical conditions and time period.

Variables	During-pre M (SD)	Post-during M (SD)	Post-pre M (SD)
STAI (State)			
Sedative	8.17 (7.65)**	−2.46 (4.94)**	5.71 (7.73)**
Stimulative	12.43 (9.18)**	−1.06 (4.34)	11.37 (9.96)**
Control	15.83 (8.42)**	−2.00 (5.67)*	13.83 (8.06)**
Systolic BP (mmHg)			
Sedative	−4.17 (5.05)**	−1.87 (3.18)**	−6.04 (5.59)**
Stimulative	−1.77 (5.83)	−1.60 (5.01)	−3.36 (7.05)**
Control	−1.68 (5.61)	−1.81 (4.97)*	−3.50 (5.21)**
Diastolic BP (mmHg)			
Sedative	−2.07 (4.76)*	−0.46 (4.26)	−2.53 (4.61)**
Stimulative	−0.62 (5.28)	−0.30 (5.50)	−0.91 (4.81)
Control	−2.78 (4.42)*	1.28 (5.28)	−1.50 (3.54)*
Heart rate (bpm)			
Sedative	−0.94 (3.62)	1.75 (4.02)*	0.81 (4.43)
Stimulative	−0.39 (5.16)	1.25 (4.65)	0.87 (4.96)
Control	0.72 (5.15)	0.73 (3.39)	1.46 (4.71)

Note: During-pre = difference in variable score collected during and pre-test; Post-during = difference in variable score collected post and during test; Post-pre = difference in variable score collected post- and pretest. *$p < .05$. **$p < .01$.

between the time periods for all conditions (all $p > .05$), with the exception of the sedative condition at the post-during time period.

For MARS, a one-way between-groups ANOVA revealed a significant effect for groups, $F(2, 102) = 4.33$, $p = .008$ (one-tailed). Post-hoc comparison using Tukey HSD revealed that the mean change scores of MARS for the sedative condition ($M = 6.06$, $SD = 10.18$) were significantly different from the no music condition ($M = 15.00$, $SD = 13.98$). There was no significant

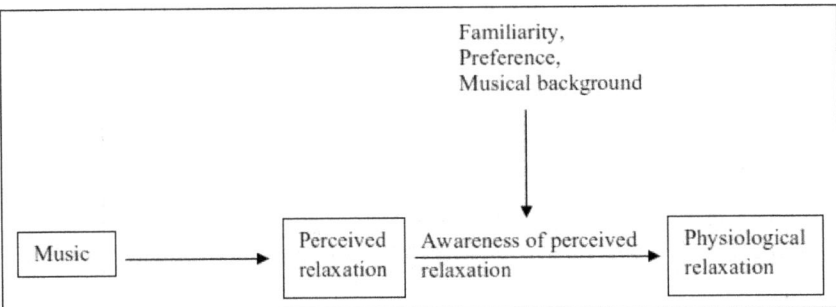

Figure 4. The Perception-to-Physiology (P2P) model.

difference between the sedative and stimulative ($M = 11.00$, $SD = 13.70$) as well as stimulative and no music condition.

Preference and familiarity

'Liking' was found by Pearson's correlation to be positively correlated with self-reported familiarity of the music, ($r = .266$, $p = .013$).

Discussion

The present study investigated the use of sedative or stimulative music to alleviate mathematics anxiety on both self-reported and physiological measures. The results of this study supported the first hypothesis that a positive correlation would be found between the self-reported measures of MARS and STAI, but rejected subsequent hypotheses that STAI and MARS would be correlated with the physiological measures of heart rate and blood pressure. The second hypothesis group was supported because the participants in the sedative music condition had lower anxiety scores than both the stimulative and no music conditions.

The positive correlation found between STAI and MARS was congruent with previous research (Ashcraft, 2002; Cemen, 1987) affirming mathematics anxiety as a bona fide subset of state anxiety. In general, we noticed a downward trend in the physiological measures with time, which may be due to the higher physiological arousal at baseline when the participants were first informed about the mathematical task.

On the whole, our results are in agreement with findings that sedative music was effective in reducing self-reported mathematics anxiety (Haynes, 2004), and that stimulative music sustained anxiety (Lingham and Theorell, 2009). Although a decrease in self-reported anxiety was found, the physiological measures appeared unaffected as previously found in a study by Lee et al. (2004). It is likely that in our study and that by Lee et al. (2004), the physiological parameters were caught at an intermediary step/ramping phase between the translation of perceived to physiological relaxation. Since further analysis (Table 3) showed pronounced systolic blood pressure changes in sedative music (supported by the similar heart rate across the musical conditions in Table 3), we propose that sedative music promoted physiological relaxation in a time-dependent and accumulative manner. We found the change in the systolic measure to be representative of blood pressure as it is clinically the more variable parameter, and diastolic pressure is generally more stable, even in pre-diseased states (Gan et al., 2003).

To explain our observation with reference to the other studies, we propose a Perception-to-Physiology (P2P) model (Figure 4) where music first reduced perceived anxiety, which would translate to physiological measures over time. This delay is likely to be more than 20 minutes, as both our study and Lee et al.'s (2004) study found self-reported relaxation without obvious physiological compliance, whereas a study by Hamel (2001) found both reported and physiological relaxation after a listening time of 20 minutes. Drawing further on the suggestion that 30 minutes was the optimal listening timeframe for anxiety management (see review by Nilsson, 2008), we propose that the inconclusive results in literature arose as a function of time in the P2P model. Perceived relaxation had to first occur before it was gradually translated into physiological relaxation after 20 minutes. The total time required for this "perception to physiology" transfer may adjust as a function of multiple factors. Here we propose that there is a threshold that the perceived anxiety must first overcome before the translation to physiological changes can be detectable (much like pain needs to reach a certain threshold before one starts screaming). On this, greater sensitivity to perceived anxiety may elicit faster physiological manifestations. This threshold is likely to be moderated by familiarity, preference, and musical training (Bernardi, Porta, and Sleight, 2006), which were found to modulate anxiety in previous studies (Bernardi et al., 2006; Lingham & Theorell, 2009).

Limitations and future directions

Whilst it is plausible that the mathematics anxiety induced in the participants is a result of the imposed time limit, our MARS findings showed that anxiety was indeed induced (shown in the correlation with STAI). Furthermore, regardless of the induction method, the anxiety fell within the operational mathematical anxiety definition of "feelings of tension and anxiety that interfered with the manipulation of numbers" (Richardson & Suinn, 1972).

Future studies may investigate alleviation of mathematics anxiety through the components of music such as major or minor keys and the valency of song lyrics. It would be useful to expand the physiological measurements to include skin conductance or salivary cortisol secretions.

Although we found a positive correlation between familiarity and preference regarding the music, we were unable to determine the relationship of these parameters to our findings. Thus we suggest that future studies may investigate a variety of music of varying familiarity in a large cohort to investigate the relationship between familiarity and preference regarding music, with that of anxiety.

Implications and conclusion

In conclusion, our study found that not all music genres reduced anxiety, and that sedative music was more effective than stimulative music in reducing mathematics anxiety through self-reports (i.e., perceived anxiety) that may lead to more pronounced subsidence of physiology. This can be beneficial because it may lead to improved mathematical performance/learning in many sectors. Our proposed P2P model explains previous discrepancies and current findings where the intermediary translation step from perceived to physiological relaxation may require at least 30 minutes for musical relaxation. Further research data on this may, in time, validate this model.

Acknowledgements

We would like to acknowledge James Cook University, Singapore, and Bioinformatics Institute, Agency for Science, Technology, and Research, Singapore, for the provision of the facilities and funding for this work.

Funding

This research received no specific grant from any funding agency in the public, commercial, or not-for-profit sectors.

References

Alexander, L., & Martray, C. (1989). The development of an abbreviated version of the mathematics anxiety rating scale. *Measurement and Evaluation in Counseling and Development, 22*(3), 143–150.

Ashcraft, M. H. (2002). Math anxiety: Personal, educational, cognitive consequences. *Current Directions in Psychological Sciences, 11*(5), 181–185. doi:10.1111/1467-8721.00196

Ashcraft, M., & Kirk, E. (2001). The relationships among working memory, math anxiety, and performance. *Journal of Experimental Psychology, 130*(2), 224–237. doi:10.1037/0096-3445.130.2.224

Baloglu, M., & Kocak, R. (2006). A multivariate investigation of the differences in mathematics anxiety. *Personality and Individual Differences, 40*(7), 1325–1335. doi:10.1016/j.paid.2005.10.009

Bernardi, L., Porta, C., & Sleight, P. (2006). Cardiovascular, cerebrovascular, and respiratory changes induced by different types of music in musicians and non- musicians: The importance of silence. *Heart, 92*(4), 445–452. doi:10.1136/hrt.2005.064600

Burns, J., Labbe, E., Williams, K., & McCall, J. (1999). Perceived and physiological indicators of relaxation: As different as Mozart and Alice in chains. *Applied Psychophysiology and Biofeedback, 24*(3), 197–202. doi:10.1023/A:1023488614364

Burns, J. L., Labbe, E., Arke, B., Capeless, K., Cooksey, B., Steadman, A., & Gonzales, C. (2002). The effects of different types of music on perceived and physiological measures of stress. *Journal of Music Therapy, 39*(2), 101–116. Retrieved from http://www.ncbi.nlm.nih.gov/pubmed

Cemen, P. B. (1987). *The nature of mathematics anxiety.* Retrieved from http://eric.ed.gov/

Chafin, S., Roy, M., Gerin, W., & Christenfeld, N. (2004). Music can facilitate blood pressure recovery from stress. *British Journal of Health Psychology, 9*(3), 393–403. doi:10.1348/1359107041557020

Clayton, M., Sager, R., & Will, U. (2005). In time with the music: The concept of entrainment and its significance for ethnomusicology. *European Meetings in Ethnomusicology, 11*, 1–82. Retrieved from http://oro.open.ac.uk

DeDonno, M., & Demaree, H. (2008). Perceived time pressure and the iowa gambling task. *Judgment and Decision Making, 3*(8), 636–640. Retrieved from http://journal.sjdm.org/

Dove, M. K. (2009). *The relationship of rhythmic and melodic perception with background music distraction in college level students.* Unpublished doctoral dissertation, University of Kansas. Retrieved from http://kuscholarworks.ku.edu/

Fonseca-Pedrero, E., Paino, M., Sierra-Baigrie, S., Lemos-Giraldez, S., & Muniz, J. (2012). Psychometric properties of the State-Trait Anxiety Inventory in college students. *Behavioral Psychology, 20*(3), 547–561.

Gadberry, A. L. (2011). Steady beat and state anxiety. *Journal of Music Therapy, 48*(3), 346–356. Retrieved from http://www.ncbi.nlm.nih.gov/pubmed

Gan, S. K. E., Loh, C. Y., & Seet, B. (2003). Hypertension in young adults an underestimated problem. *Singapore Medical Journal, 44*(9), 448–452.

Hamel, W. J. (2001). The effects of music intervention on anxiety in patient waiting for cardiac catheterization. *Intensive and Critical Care Nursing, 17*(5), 279–285. doi:10.1054/iccn.2001.1594

Hardie, M. J. (1990). *The effect of music on mathematics anxiety and achievement* (Doctoral dissertation). Retrieved from Proquest Dissertations and Theses database. (UMI No. 9032555)

Haynes, S. E. (2004). *The effects of background music on the mathematics test anxiety of college algebra students* (Doctoral dissertation). Retrieved from PsycINFO. (2004-99021-046)

Hishinuma, E. S., Goebert, D. A., Guerrero, A. P., Miyamoto, R. H., Nishimura, S. T., Nahulu, L. B., et al. (2000). Psychometric properties of the state-trait anxiety inventory for Asian/Pacific-islander adolescents. *Assessment, 7*(1), 17–36. doi:10.1177/107319110000700102

Hooper, J. (2012). Predictable factors in sedative music: A tool to identify sedative music for receptive music therapy. *Australian Journal of Music Therapy, 23*, 59–74. Retrieved from http://search.informit.com.au/

Jones, G. (2001). Applying psychology to the teaching of basic math: A case study. *Inquiry, 6*(2), 60–65. Retrieved from http://eric.ed.gov/

Knight, W. E. J., & Rickard, N. S. (2001). Relaxing music prevents stress-induced increases in subjective anxiety, systolic blood pressure, and heart rate in healthy males and females. *Journal of Music Therapy, 38*(4), 254–272. Retrieved from http://www.ncbi.nlm.nih.gov/pubmed

Labbe, E., Schmidt, N., Babin, J., & Pharr, M. (2007). Coping with stress: The effectiveness of different types of music. *Applied Psychophysiology and Biofeedback, 32*(3–4), 163–168. doi:10.1007/s10484-007-0943-9

Lee, D., Henderson, A., & Shum, D. (2004). The effect of music on preprocedure anxiety in Hong Kong Chinese day patients. *Journal of Clinical Nursing, 13*(3), 297–303. doi:10.1046/j.1365-2702.2003.00888.x

Lingham, J., & Theorell, T. (2009). Self-selected "favourite" stimulative and sedative music listening: How does familiar and preferred music listening affect the body? *Nordic Journal of Music Therapy, 18*(2), 150–166. doi:10.1080/08098130903062363

Mattarella-Micke, A., Mateo, J., Kozak, M. N., Foster, K., & Beilock, S. L. (2011). Choke or thrive? The relationship between salivary cortisol and math performance depends on individual differences in working memory and math anxiety. *Emotion, 11*(4), 1000–1005. doi:10.1037/a0023224

McCroskey, J. C. (1997). Self-report measurement. In J. A. Daly, J. C. McCroskey, J. Ayres, T. Hopf & D. Sonandre (Eds.), *Avoiding communication: Shyness, reticence, and communication apprehension* (pp. 191–216). Cresskill, NJ: Hampton Press.

Nilsson, U. (2008). The anxiety and pain reducing effects of music interventions: A systematic review. *Aorn Journal, 87*(4), 780–807. doi:10.1016/j.aorn.2007.09.013

Pelletier, C. L. (2004). The effect of music on decreasing arousal due to stress: A meta-analysis. *Journal of Music Therapy, 41*(3), 192–214. Retrieved from http://www.ncbi.nlm.nih.gov/pubmed

Plake, B. S., & Parker, C. S. (1982). The development and validation of a revised version of the mathematics anxiety rating scale. *Educational and Psychological Measurement, 42*(2), 551–557. doi:10.1177/001316448204200218

Richardson, F. C., & Suinn, R. M. (1972). The mathematic anxiety rating scale: Psychometric data. *Journal of Counseling Psychology, 19*(6), 551–554. doi:10.1037/h0033456

Sheffield, D., & Hunt, T. (2006). How does anxiety influence maths performance and what can we do about it? *MSOR Connections, 6*(4), 19–23. doi:10.11120/msor.2006.06040019

Spielberger, C. D., Gorsuch, R. L., & Lushene, R. E. (1970). *The State-Trait Anxiety Inventory test manual.* Palo Alto, CA: Consulting Psychologist Press.

Walworth, D. D. (2003). The effect of preferred music genre selection versus preferred song selection on experimentally induced anxiety levels. *Journal of Music Therapy, 40*(1), 2–14. Retrieved from http://www.ncbi.nlm.nih.gov/pubmed

Yew, S.H., Lim, K.M.J., Haw, Y.X., & Gan, S.K.E. (2015). The Interaction between perceived stress, optimisim, life satisfaction and physical health in the Singaporean Asian context. *Asian Journal of Humanities and Social Sciences, 3*(1). Retrieved from http://ajhss.org/pdfs/Vol3Issue1/7.pdf

Yun, X. (2013a). *Pass GCE O level examination: Additional mathematics by topic.* Singapore: Shinglee Publishers.

Yun, X. (2013b). *Pass GCE O level examination: Mathematics by topic.* Singapore: Shinglee Publishers.

Article 3: Self-Analysis in the 16th century Reformation

October 2017 marks the 500th year since the start of the Reformation, usually attributed to start when Martin Luther nailed his thesis onto the church door to call all true believers of the Lord Jesus Christ to reaffirm the need for constant correction of our erring ways. While the actual reformation started before Luther, at the time of Wycliffe and some say Erasmus, there is no doubt that the Lord's hand is behind it all, for the church had erred into superstition and human traditions away from the Truth of God's Words in the Bible.

We often read about the "heroic" display of unwavering steadfastness of the reformer even unto death (e.g., Tyndale who started the translation of the Bible into vernacular English and was burnt to death). Yet in all their heroics, their mistakes also teach us the need to be humble. In their steadfastness, many of these reformers have gotten stubborn and made grave mistakes What is the guide to prevent making these mistakes?

Humility, discernment and absolute obedience to God's Word.

There are some who claim to let our conscience be our guide and quote Romans 2:15 - Which shew the work of the law written in their hearts, their conscience also bearing witness, and their thoughts the mean while accusing or else excusing one another;

Yet, how reliable is the human conscience? For whatever wrong these reformers did, they did according to their conscience and that certainly did not stop them from making grave mistakes. Let us not forget

Jeremiah 17:9 - The heart is deceitful above all things, and desperately wicked: who can know it?

And in reference to Mark Owen's writing on the psychology of sin, we fallen creatures are certainly very good at justifying even our wrongs.

"Now sin, when it presseth upon the soul to this purpose, will use a thousand wiles to hide from it the terror of the Lord, the end of transgressions, and especially of that peculiar folly which it solicits the mind unto. Hopes of pardon shall be used to hide it; and future repentance shall hide it; and present importunity of lust shall hide it; occasions and opportunities shall hide it; surprisals shall hide it; extenuation of sin shall hide it; balancing of duties against it shall hide it; fixing the imagination on present objects shall hide it; desperate resolutions to venture the uttermost for the enjoyment of lust in its pleasures and profits shall hide it. A thousand wiles it hath, which cannot be recounted."

John Owen's Remainders of Indwelling Sin in Believers

For explanation, let us look at the few examples.

Martin Luther nailed his thesis onto the church door. Yet let us not forget that he had a major disagreement with the Swiss Reformer Zwingli because he held on to the erroneous doctrine of consubstantiation. He misapplied "biblical separation" and erred much in his ways of holding onto the non-biblical doctrine on consubstantiation. Did he not know the verse that Jesus said, "in remembrance" (Luke 22:19 and 1 Corinthians 11:24)? He knew, but his eyes were clouded, perhaps by his self-righteousness (a trap that many who are godly fall in. E.g., Moses in Numbers 20:12; Isaiah in 1 Kings 18:22 where he believed that the Lord left only him). By Luther's own conscience he did right but he certainly was not.

Another example, Zwingli himself persecuted the Anabaptists to even death because they held on to full immersion for baptism. Again, his application of biblical separation or insisting on what is right was misapplied leading to the persecution and deaths of fellow believers over self-imposed dogmatic views. In doing so he had basically blood on his hands.

During World War 2, Bonhoeffer the great German pastor of Hitler's time, called for the lesser of 2 evils and the assassination of Hitler. Bonhoeffer conveniently suppressed the Decalogue commandment on killing. And let us not forget that Hitler also justified the persecution of Jews using Martin Luther's anti-Semitic views.

Great people of God, erring in their clear conscience do not make wrong deeds right. They lacked humility, discernment, and obedience to God's Word at the point in time. Bonhoeffer ignored that "Thou shalt not kill" included both in direct and indirect killing. There was no doubt that the reformers and Bonhoeffer are great men of God, and they did great things, but they also erred, often in more than mild inconsequential sins.

Let us never rely on our conscience alone but solely on the careful study of God's Word in humility, with discernment and absolute obedience to His Word. Our conscience, being part of us, is also fallen, and is used as a tool by the Holy Ghost in our sanctification, to lead us to repentance. And our hearts, where our conscience is implied to reside in by its Chinese name 良心, is deceitful in itself. In fact, Romans 2:15 refers to our conscience as witnesses to our own fallen nature, not necessary as the judge. And if we cannot get by our own conscience, can we expect to get by before the One True Judge? Clearly, there is only one solution as mentioned in the following verse.

Proverbs 3:5-6 - Trust in the Lord with all your heart, and do not lean on your own understanding. In all your ways acknowledge him, and he will make straight your paths.

Article 4: A testimony of what the various disciplines led a sinner to see the Truth of the Bible

Below is a list of academic fields that I have dabbled in, and what they have shown me about the Truth of God's Word.

Discipline: Biosciences, Biomedical Sciences
Points of appreciation: Creation, wonders of His creations, and His sovereignty in them. He alone is the Healer and Scientist. We just discover and use what He had created. The importance of DNA, RNA and Protein shows the importance of every jot and tittle of God's Word.

Discipline: Translation & Interpretation.
Points of appreciation: The beauty of language and interpretation. Bible translations, their purity and corruptions.

Discipline: Psychology.
Points of appreciation: The state of the fallen world, & how we love, worship and justify sin e.g. we lie constantly.

Discipline: Business Admin.
Points of appreciation: The management of this created world by God; the rules and law set by God, the Mosaic law, the management of the Hebrews in the Pentateuch, and church management in the New Testament.

Discipline: Complexity Science.

Points of appreciation: The interconnectedness of God's mysteries and His creations. Ultimately His sovereignty. We are all creations. How one's sin or holy deed can spread like yeast.

Discipline: Law.

Points of appreciation: The purpose and beauty of the Mosaic Law, salvation, justification, sanctification, redemption and sin.

Discipline: Theology

Points of appreciation: Tying in all the above and seeing how they are all inspired from the Bible, and originate from God. The Ultimate authority of the Bible and God's words in our created world, but God Himself is Supreme over everything including the Bible. And also to see how the above disciplines got twisted in the fallen world to their current state.

What little dabbling I had in interior design and architecture also allowed me to better appreciate the instructions in the building of Solomon's Temple to God and Noah's Ark.

There is no doubt that every discipline and all knowledge only helps to appreciate the mysteries and wonders of God's creation.

What is your field? What is your appreciation of the Bible and what was to be done in today's world?

Article 5: Stockholm syndrome and the election of God

Many negotiators and psychologists would be very familiar with the Stockholm syndrome (named after a bank robbery in Stockholm in 1973 where hostages sided with the bank robbers against their rescuers, see https://en.wikipedia.org/wiki/Stockholm_syndrome). FBI estimates 8% of hostages to exhibit such bizarre behavior in liking their captivity and hate being rescued. Yet this phenomenon may well be more prevalent and well-documented than expected.

In the Christian world, how many of us actually prefer to keep sinning and would actually hold a grudge against God for His good laws and salvation? While it may sound preposterous to the average Christian at first thought, this is actually evident from our unrepentant behaviors, where we continuously indulge in sin repeatedly. .

In the Stockholm robbery, the hostages, despite being kept captive for six days by bank robbers, sympathized with the robbers because of the lack of abuse. While it truly is nice to not be abused, they forgot they were held against their will in a bank. They hated the rescuers and even defended the robbers when the law enforcers broke in. In such odd behavior, they forgot about their family and friends waiting outside in worry for them.

Are we not like that in Christianity? The world holds us captive, but does not abuse all of us. In fact, many of us in developed nations lead relatively comfortable carnal lives. While many of us will protest that we did not reject salvation. But on deeper analysis, we actually had.

In fact, this rejection was also recorded in the Bible. After the Hebrews were delivered from Egypt, did they not say to elect another leader to return to Egypt (Numbers 14:4)? Did God not rebuke Israel for rejecting Him in Jeremiah 1:16; 2:21; 3:20; 15:6; 31:32; Hosea 11:1-4; Deuteronomy

32:18; Ezra 8:22; Leviticus 26:27-28; 2 Chronicles 36:16; Proverbs 1:24-26)?

In the New Testament, did we not do the same? (Romans 2:8; John 12:48; Matthew 10:33; Luke 12:9; Luke 9:26) amongst the many other verses. We are a wicked generation, often seeking signs from God (Matthew 16:4) for our faith. We ask God to show us this and that, but few would prostrate before God to ask Him to help our unbelief (Mark 9:24). Despite the Lord pouring down His Word, mercy and love on us, we have refused (Proverbs 1:24-25), pursuing our own ways (Proverbs 1:31) chasing after atheism, the theory of evolution, aliens, and vain superstitions. To feel better, we compromise and try and fit our idea of God with these vain philosophies and practices.

We are exhibiting the Stockholm syndrome. We have sided with the world and the Devil. Little wonder that we are by default, the children of the devil (John 8:44). We have refused His outreached hand and given Word to us. Like the hostages that not only shunned rescue but hated their rescuers, mankind has hated God and shunned His salvation. We question why it has to be His way. Why there cannot be another way to heaven. We question His right to rescue us. Certainly, we deserve absolute annihilation for our foolish choices to love our captors. We are so depraved and so unable to help ourselves that we have no choice but to rely on His election (Calvin's Institutes – Total Depravity, and Unconditional Election). Just as the police had to rescue the hostages by force and against their will, we need the election of God to wake us up from our foolishness. We will scream that we did not ask for help because we are so lost in the Stockholm syndrome of the world, that our loving God had to predestine us for our sakes (Romans 8:29). And yet in this, the patience of the Lord is beyond our comprehension. Some of us, elected to receive His Word, still choose to wallow in our sin like "a dog that returns to its vomit" or "the sow that returns to wallowing in the mire" (2 Peter 2:22). It is akin to those whom the police had rescued but still choose to return to a state of captivity. The Stockholm syndrome is clearly only part of the Fallen Man syndrome.

Let us who are illuminated by His Word to see our own foolishness, repent and forsake our sins. Let us turn to Him in humility and ask for His forgiveness and thank Him for not leaving us to our foolishness. For great is His love, His patience, and His salvation.

Article 6: Psychological tests and Intelligent Design

The below article was published in the Creation Magazine in 2015. In this article, I pointed out the illogical conclusion of atheists to deny and dismiss the evidence of not only intelligence, but also of planning, power, and wisdom simply from the observation of the natural world around us.

Romans 1:20 - For the invisible things of him from the creation of the world are clearly seen, being understood by the things that are made, even his eternal power and Godhead; so that they are without excuse:

If atheists can accept the use of games, such as the Tower of Hanoi to measure human intelligence, why is it that the more complex world is not a testament of God's creation?

Similarly, if the 64 disc version of this game, based on relatively known simple set of rules can take 585 billion years to complete, how can one believe that the natural world, being in magnitudes more complex, take ~15 billion years by chance?

Clearly, in denying God, they have easily reveled in their own illogical contradictions.

Romans 1:21-22 – Because that, when they knew God, they glorified him not as God, neither were thankful; but became vain in their imaginations, and their foolish heart was darkened. Professing themselves to be wise, they became fools.

THE TOWER OF HANOI

A TEST OF DESIGN, PLANNING, AND PURPOSE

The famous Kashi Vishwanath Temple in Varanasi, in the Indian state of Uttar Pradesh, is regarded as one of the holiest places in Hinduism. Various legends involving Brahma, the Hindu deity of creation, associate this temple with a form of the puzzle featured here.

Samuel Gan

THE TOWER of Hanoi, also known as Lucas's tower[1] or the Tower of Brahma, is a game or puzzle requiring considerable skill and mental aptitude. By assessing the number of steps one takes to move the discs to another pole while following certain rules, this game tests one's cognitive functioning as well as programming skills.

It eventually became included in the Cambridge Neuropsychological Test Automated Battery (CANTAB) developed in the 1980s to measure memory, attention, reaction time, decision making, and response control.[2]

Used by many psychologists today, the game, as is suggested by its multiple names, appears to have its roots within varying cultures. It is also an unspoken testament that all we know of could only have been created by an all-powerful, super-intelligent God.

Nothing to everything, by itself?

Atheistic evolutionists believe that our world came from nothing. And they believe that later, whatever something there was organized itself by random processes, constrained only by the physical laws, to form the complex world around us. Since they insist that no supernatural intelligence was involved, and since this world is indeed very complex, they believe that billions of years are required in order for chance to make these complex systems possible.

But randomness does not observe rules,[3] whereas such rules are all around us. Seashells, trees and many other things in the natural world grow in patterns that follow the mathematical Fibonacci sequence.[4] All of life follows the highly complicated processes of DNA replication, transcription, and translation.

There is a rule of life, known as the Law of Biogenesis; life only ever comes from life. No matter has ever been observed to assemble itself into anything approaching the complexity of even the simplest living thing.[5]

Life is full of ordered processes with rules and sequential order governing them. The first self-reproducing entity in evolution could not have had the help of any selection or mutation, because natural selection only applies to living things. Therefore only chance can be invoked. But for pure chance to build the sorts of systems required for a self-reproducing organism, not even 'zillions' of years would be plausible, much less the few billion years pushed by evolutionists.

To highlight this, consider the following. According to one legend, there is a room in the Hindu temple of Kashi Vishwanath in India with three rods and 64 golden discs, said to be moved by Brahmin priests according to the rules of this puzzle. (This is a possible explanation for the name 'Tower of Brahma'.) Let's assume we were to move these 64 discs at a rate of one disc per second, and by applying very high intelligence,

---

"All of life follows the highly complicated processes of DNA replication, transcription, and translation."

---

we were to ensure that the smallest number of moves is required. It would still take 18,446,744,073,709,551,615 turns or 585 billion years—some 40 times longer than the assumed evolutionary age of the whole universe!

Imagine how inconceivably much longer it would take for *chance* to achieve

TESTING BRAINPOWER

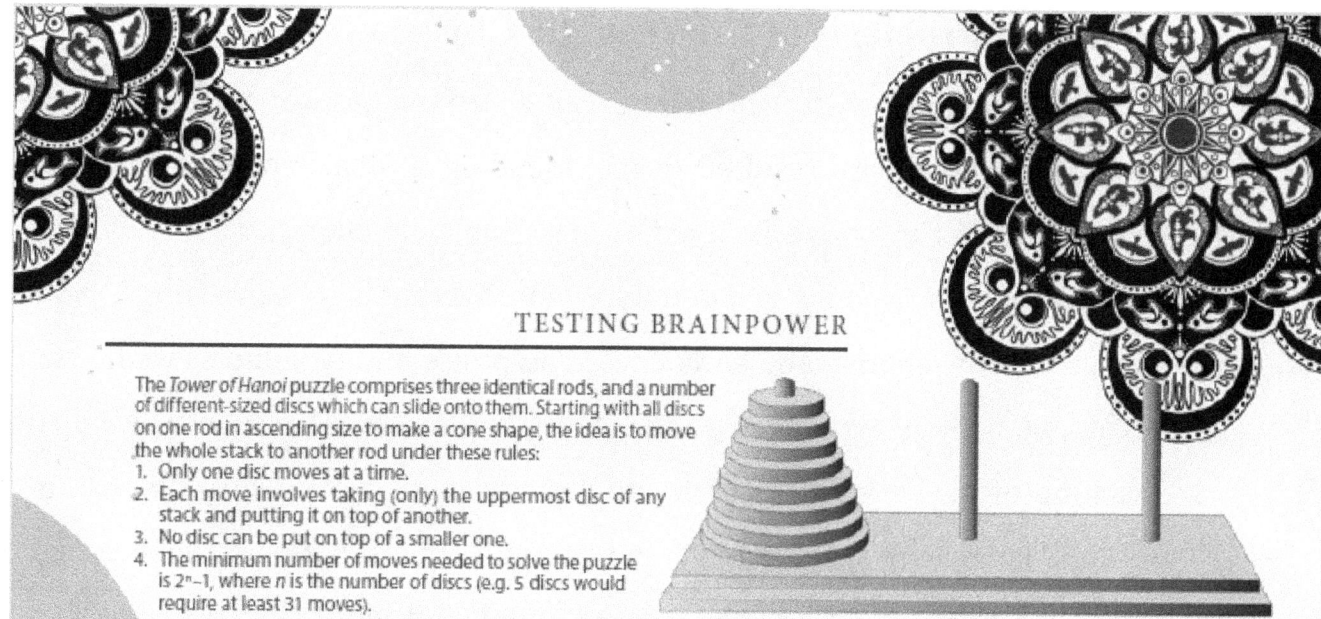

The *Tower of Hanoi* puzzle comprises three identical rods, and a number of different-sized discs which can slide onto them. Starting with all discs on one rod in ascending size to make a cone shape, the idea is to move the whole stack to another rod under these rules:
1. Only one disc moves at a time.
2. Each move involves taking (only) the uppermost disc of any stack and putting it on top of another.
3. No disc can be put on top of a smaller one.
4. The minimum number of moves needed to solve the puzzle is 2^n-1, where n is the number of discs (e.g. 5 discs would require at least 31 moves).

---

this same solution in, say, a situation in which the choice of disc were random, with no intelligence or intelligent programming to be able to ensure the smallest number of turns.

Small wonder that the legend states that the tower was created at the beginning of the world, and that the world would end when the puzzle was completed. Yet any of the basic processes required of life, such as DNA replication, transcription, and protein translation, easily outstrip the complexity of the Tower of Hanoi task—by orders of magnitude.[6]

Time related to intelligence

Furthermore, since the time (and number of moves) taken to complete the Tower of Hanoi task gives some idea of a person's cognitive capabilities, having all of creation made in just six days tells us of God's unfathomable power and intelligence.

For any creative task, whether solving a puzzle, making a table or indeed a universe, the more power and intelligence that is at work, the shorter the time needed—and vice versa. Thus, for a very gifted adult, figuring out the Tower of Hanoi solution for a handful of discs might take only a few hours at most.[7] Yet the same solution might readily take the average seven-year-old (assuming no lapse in concentration, ever) every waking hour of ten years.

Had God used evolution, and taken billions of years to create as theistic evolutionists believe, it would clearly rob Him of His glory. The all-powerful, all-intelligent God Who created time itself could even have accomplished all of creation in 'no time' if He had so wished.[8]

The Tower of Hanoi is generally accepted as a cognitive test by psychologists, many of whom are atheists. It is a wonder that they cannot see that all of creation, being much more wonderfully structured and with processes that require much more complex 'instructions' than are needed to solve this puzzle, is a huge testament to God's power and His creative designing intelligence.

Samuel Gan, B.Sc., AKC, AHEA, MBPsS, Ph.D
Dr Gan is a biomedical scientist and an undergraduate psychology research supervisor. He is also the co-developer of DNAApp, a mobile app for analysis of DNA sequences, and is a member of the Singapore Friends of CMI.

References and notes

1. After French mathematician Édouard Lucas who popularized this puzzle in the late 1800s, and is known for his study of Fibonacci sequences (see Ref. 4.)
2. The CANTAB can use either the Tower of Hanoi or its simplified cousin, the 'Tower of London', which is thought to give a "purer test of planning ability"—see Ozonoff, S. *et al*, Performance on Cambridge Neuropsychological test automated battery subtests sensitive to frontal lobe function in people with autistic disorder: Evidence from the collaborative programs of excellence in autism network, *Journal of Autism and Developmental Disorders* 34(3):139–150, 2004.
3. Macroscopic systems do reflect the 'rules' of probability applied to large numbers of random processes; see Wieland, C., *World Winding Down: a layman's guide to the Second Law of Thermodynamics*, Creation Book Publishers, Powder Springs, GA 2013.
4. Wieland, C., and Grigg, R., Golden numbers, *Creation* 16(4):26, 1994; creation.com/golden.
5. Dr Craig Venter did create a simple form of synthetic life, but this involved huge amounts of directed intelligence in copying the original design. See Sarfati, J., Was life really created in a test tube? And does it disprove biblical creation? creation.com/venter, 25 May 2010.
6. Thus by 10, 100, 1,000, 10,000 times or more.
7. This assumes they are unaware of the various 'rules' for its inevitable solution others have calculated.
8. The obvious question is, 'Why then did He take six days?' The answer seems to be found in Exodus 20:11 (part of the Ten Commandments delivered to the Israelites), where the six days of God's work and one day of rest are given as the basis for man's work and rest in the Sabbath Commandment.

> "More power and intelligence that is at work, the shorter the time needed"

Article 7: Problems of Charismatic Christianity

I grew up a Presbyterian church. But a combination of laziness and the moving of the church resulted in me attending a local independent church that was nearer to where I stayed at that time. The church was lively, filed more with young people, and certainly more vibrant and "happening". It was a church with "charismatic" practices. The praise and worship sessions were great but without reverence to the Most High God. It also was weak on teaching of God's word. There were periods of mass tongue (gibberish, not foreign language) speaking, yet never with interpretation. The messages were generally based on testimonies, often edifying the speaker. These sessions were called "sharing", and occasionally there were self-claimed prophets that came as guest speakers. I attended the church for almost ten years of my life, yet my knowledge of God hardly grew. Rather, my superstitions grew, with increasing fear of demons, idols, spiritual bondages and the likes.

There were times during these ten years where I debated with people in the church on tongues speaking and the miraculous healings. Despite being in such a church for ten years, God preserved me, yet this preservation also resulted in many disagreements with people in the church, especially when I pointed out that the practice of mass speaking in tongues did not even fit orderly worship in 1 Corinthians 13.

When I left the church for overseas study, I joined a lovely fundamental Baptist church, yet it was not free from the influence of charismatism in Hillsong songs. While tongues speaking were not practiced, there were charismatic elements as the pastor believed in private practice of tongues. This led me to wonder if there were biblical basis for the speaking in tongues. How many interpretations of certain scriptures are there? Is everyone right? Even when the interpretations conflict? There must be only ONE interpretation. What did God exactly say in the scriptures regarding tongues speaking? Is it gibberish or foreign languages? What does the context say?

Perhaps to first address the speaking of tongues, nowhere does the Bible record the speaking of gibberish. The Pentecost was when the apostles spoke in a language that sounded native to the listeners. Attempts to claim that the practice today referred to angelic tongues, is also nonsensical as in all appearances of angels, from Old Testament records to the events recorded in the book of Revelation, nowhere did the angels speak in languages that were not somehow understandable to the listeners. In claims of it as groaning, there was again no record of any prophet or apostle, filled with the Spirit, groaning en masse. In serious study of the Scripture, there is indeed no evidence of gibberish speaking en masse that did not make sense to the listeners. To what scriptural basis there is for the phenomenon, there is none. What it is in essence, is the mental tripping of the tongue in attempting to enunciate rapid fire words in succession in a form of stammering. There has been no evidence in Scripture where such ability had conferred any specific Holy Spirit gifts as often claimed by proponents of the movement to be a sign of Holy Spirit indwelling and filling.

The other hallmark of Charismatism in miraculous healing appealed much more to me. As someone who had severe childhood asthma and allergies, there was no shortage of me attending "healing sessions" by "prophets" in the Singapore charismatic churches. In some of these special meetings, "prophets" came and gave talks, mostly on their experience with a couple of bible verses interspersed if any. Some had outrageous claims that Christ Himself was standing next to them. Some pointed to the audience, claiming that God told them that someone was afflicted with some situation and that God had "a word of comfort for them". This method of "prophecy" employed by these "prophets" was not too far from "cold reading" whenever they claimed to have a word from God about someone in the congregation being afflicted with some unfortunate event. In a large enough group, it is obvious that "God told me one of you had an unhappy experience, a break up or losing a loved one" would certainly strike a chord with someone. Even as a kid then, I would pray silently, "Lord, if this man is truly a prophet, let him single me out for my disbelief at his claim." So far, no "prophet" ever singled me out even after staring right at my face.

In some of these miraculous healing sessions, I went forward to the "altar", and was pushed very hard on my head though I never did fall back. I never felt the need to. Searching the scriptures, there was no record of such practices in the miraculous healings by Christ or any prophet or apostle.

I do remember one particular event where the visiting "prophet" was rumored to be able to know the problem without being told. That remained a rumor. I prayed for healing, but I also prayed that God heal me completely, including a bad cut on my finger. I thought at that time that it would not make sense if God would heal me of my allergies but leave me shortsighted and also with my cut on my finger. After the session, I was still shortsighted. Neither did the cut miraculously heal. The "prophet" merely said a general healing prayer for me.

In some of these healing sessions, I was put under the impression that on top of my lack of faith, which was responsible for my resistance to miraculous healing, was that I could have been plagued by some spiritual bondage or demonically plagued like Saul. Therefore, in some of these healing sessions, it was almost like an exorcism where the healer attempts to "bind" the demon responsible for the disease state. In all these, I was confused further. Was I possessed in some form thus I was plagued with allergies? Why were the exorcisms ineffective? Is the name of the Lord Jesus Christ without power to heal or cast out the demon? Could the demon possess a professing believer?

There were more questions than answers. And a very poor and wrong understanding of God pushed me further from the truth.

As I got serious in my faith, I enrolled myself in proper biblical teaching and scientific investigations. It is only then that I understood that there was always a component of placebo effect or psychosomatic medicine. The psychosomatic medicinal effects were often temporary at best, especially when under excitement, some disabled or injured individual who could not normally walk, could take some small steps. There is little difference from the "fight or flight" response where under heightened senses of danger, there is an outburst of superhuman energy. This has been observed with mothers when their children were in danger, and the mothers lifted items that they usually could not, or they performed other superhuman feats of physical activity. It is what is commonly termed as adrenalin rush. However, true healing from the Bible accounts were immediate and not temporary. The lame did walk, and they did so for a good long time, and certainly not with a limp. To date, despite my numerous attendances in these healing sessions, I have yet to see any complete and miraculous healing of anyone that went forward, even by "prophets with special gifts of healing". What was even laughable was that the blame for the lack of healing was never upon the healer, but always the folks seeking healing for lacking faith. This is in direct contradiction to the unbelieving father of the possessed child asking for the Lord Jesus' exorcism in Mark 9:23-25. Was the healing in this account subject to the father's belief? Or was it due to the possessed child's belief? In fact, in Acts, the apostles healed many who did not recognize them as apostles. Wherein was the source of faith for healing? Such nonsense on the lack of miracles because of the lack of faith of the sick is an excuse by these false healers. Can the Lord heal? Certainly, He does today on the sick through prayer, often through medical knowledge given to man. There are certainly miraculous healings that happen in the corner of the bed through fervent prayer of true believers. Yet to expect the special signs and wonders of a specific healer like in the apostolic times, is clearly a thing of the past.

The same it is today that there are no more demonic possessions or exorcisms. As taught in Chin Lien Bible Seminary, there are no demonic possessions recorded after the time of the Acts of the Apostles. Neither was the topic of demonic possession, an important issue discussed in the epistles for the early church. Certainly, it is an important area, but amazingly, there is no Mosaic Law particularly dealing with demonic possessions and the Scriptures outside the areas of Christ Himself addressing it. Perhaps the most convincing case is that even in the end times when Satan could run amok as recorded in the book of Revelation, there are no demonic possession cases. One would also find a lack of examples of demonic possessions in the Old Testament. A careful reading of the account of Saul, his illness and the encounter with the Witch of Endor will reveal that they are not possessions. In fact, demon possessions were only recorded in the time of Christ and of the apostles.

Nonetheless, even if one finds the cessation of demonic possessions controversial, illnesses are clearly not only due to demonic possessions. The women with the issue of blood, the lame, the blind, and the other numerous examples in the scriptures did not have demonic possession causes. Should a demon be behind it as in the case of Saul or Job, it is permitted by God for His purposes. On this point, one cannot possibly exorcise their physical ailments away just as Job would not be healed of Satan's afflictions through an exorcism. It is allowed by God for God's glory. Not recognizing so is again putting up unbiblical understanding of God's sovereignty.

The other problem of charismatic Christianity is Prosperity gospel (discussed in Another Practical Guide, Article 9). The lack of control over who goes onto the pulpit in many cases can lead to such nonsense being preached. God is certainly not a fool, and certainly not a foolish banker. Would God not know the wickedness of man's hearts to give more in order to receive more? The doctrine had tainted the will and desire of many who would have given willingly. And certainly, God does not need or want our money nor our belief nor attendance to be God. He is not the "god of fortune" or "Tinkerbell" from Peter Pan, requiring belief from people to gain power or energy, and certainly, God does not promise a 1000% interest rate on your investment for His work. The prosperity gospel doctrine has played on human greed, poisoning the desire to give, and also as a means for swindlers to cheat the hard earned money of believers into giving more than they can. It also puts God to a test to provide for the greedy since they did it out of "a pure heart". Oh the great poison in a charismatic church, that I can no longer mince my words but call it a great "swindling" attempt. Is God so early swindled? Certainly the Lord rewards and give to those that give with a pure and sincere heart (Malachi 3:10), but certainly not at the expectation of God giving you back more.

The danger of these issues are that the years of lacking clarity on these, compounded by the false "prophets" and not being healed, led to my disappointment at a straw man God. It was only through proper biblical teaching that I realized how I had wasted years away in failing to learn God's Word and cast down false images of God.

Charismatism and the associated movements (Pentacostalism, Power evangelism, etc) are very dangerous movements in Christianity. They not only set up a false view on God away from the Truth as revealed by the Lord Himself in the Scriptures, they offer false hopes of salvation, and also set up disappointments in God when "prophets" and "healings" fail. While there are certainly saved individuals amidst such movements, it is a treacherous ground to be treading. It is better to be as biblical as possible than to err, for we are before the One Holy God Who has revealed what He expects of us in the Bible, and revealing His character.

Article 8: Speaking/Teaching animals in the Bible

Can man speak to animals as depicted in the great classic "The Chronicles of Narnia" by CS Lewis?

No.

The few biblical records of speaking animals were those of special miraculous situations. The snake tempted Eve in Eden, the donkey reasoned with Balaam, otherwise you do not get speech from the snake or donkey at the zoo.

One might get a parrot once that has severely limited speech once in a while, but we can certainly agree that animals do not generally reason with humans nor discuss knowledge and philosophy. Not even the smart Lucy, a chimpanzee that mastered sign language is not capable of reasoning like the Eden snake or Balaam's donkey.

https://en.m.wikipedia.org/wiki/Lucy_(chimpanzee)

A study of biology and psychology have shown that generally, the snake or donkey does not have the vocal structure nor the language cognition capabilities to articulate human speech in the very same way humans speak to one another. Those recorded in the Bible are unique special situations, particular Balaam's donkey, where God decided to open the mouth of the animal to teach Balaam. If they generally could speak, it would not be a miracle anyway. On the Eden snake, man was perfect before the Fall, so it is possible that there was some non-language communication between Eve and the snake of some sort, as people can, to a limited extent, understand their pets. Nonetheless, we should not expect animals to reason or tempt us.

Yet, the Bible teaches that all creation testifies of His creation. Do we then speak to animals?

Job 12:7-9 : But ask the beasts, and they will teach you; the birds of the heavens, and they will tell you; Or speak to the earth, and it shall teach thee: and the fishes of the sea shall declare unto thee. Who knoweth not in all these that the hand of the LORD hath wrought this?

Let us read the verse carefully, there is no part that suggest that the beasts or birds or fishes would speak to us even though they will teach us. So how would they generally teach us the hand of God?

Their declaration of the animals are in what they do everyday. They constantly declare. Their very beings and existence declare God's creation. We can study them physiologically, psychologically, and by every method known to man and we will see God's handiwork.

This is perhaps one of the few verse that supports for the scientific study of zoology and aquaculture and all the related scientific disciplines like molecular biology, animal psychology, and even animal linguistics.

Understanding the world around us is important is appreciating God's majesty!!

Article 9: Loose Language

It is increasingly evident that the attacks of Satan unto the languages of man is an attack to God's Word. Truly, Satan's attack is multi-pronged in approach. Apart from the well-established attack on the Masoretic Text and Textus Receptus through the corrupted versions and "older" versions like the corrupted Septuagint of the Old Testament, and the Sinaiticus and Vaticanus for the New Testament, the obvious attack that Satan has also mounted is on the language of man. Classical languages are now replaced by modern versions. Most obvious in this writing here is the use of English. The plurality of 'you' is made confusion from the more classical "thee", "ye", "thou", etc. Meanings of words have changed where from originally referring to the people, the word 'church' is now often used for buildings. To make matters worse, many have adopted a very loose use of language, often using the wrong words or meanings. While such problems are less pronounced among academic fields, the problem is rampant in general use. In other cultures, words no longer reflect what is said, and most people speak flippantly, idly, and things that no longer mean what was conveyed. For example, when food is offered in many Asian communities, it is cultural to put on an act of politeness to refuse when they actually mean the contrary. When confronted if it is lying, it is often excused as a cultural norm or necessary for the social context. "No thanks" no longer means a negative response, but can now be taken as dependent on situations to range from politeness, flat refusal, to an excuse.

However the Bible clearly teaches in Matthew 5:37 - But let your communication be, Yea, yea; Nay, nay: for whatsoever is more than these cometh of evil.

To idly gossip, speak flippantly, are not biblically good behaviors as well. The Bible clearly teaches in Matthew 12:36 - But I say unto you, That every idle word that men shall speak, they shall give account thereof in the day of judgment.

The degradation of language is obvious in today's world. The repetitious use of words by the aged, the flippancy and idle words of the average man, are all just some further examples that clearly erode not only understanding of languages on the whole, but to subconsciously cause man to doubt God's Word. For when man becomes accustomed to idle and meaningless words spoken by one another, they are trained to react in the same manner to biblical forthtelling or when they read the Scriptures.

Even in the field of academia, there are pointless idles words written and spoken in academic writings and presentations. In the midst of all these attack on man's understanding of God's word, it is truly the anointing of the Holy Ghost to teach man that they need to learn to communicate properly, most importantly when listening, forthtelling, and reading the very word of God. For it alone has the authority.

May the Lord God continue to guide us and preserve us, for the effects of the Fall have clear implications even in our understanding and handling of the Word of God.

Article 10: Demonology

This article stems from my search within the scriptures of the various issues of Demonology. Extra biblical sources are not referred to. This is also an add on to the issue of exorcism as discussed earlier in Charismatism.

Demons are fallen angels (Revelation 12). There is controversy here to what are all the reasons for the fall of angels, although it is well accepted that pride and arrogance leading to mutiny as the reason (see Ezekiel 28 and Revelation 12:4). Yet, there are some that believe that Genesis 6 also shows the falling when they have offspring with the daughters of man.

As already discussed in "A Guide to the Biblical Lands – Article 6", the son of God, in context of "kind after kind" and Jesus' explanation of angels being somewhat asexual (Matthew 22:30), and in agreement of Romans 8, the "sons of God", are referring to humans, likely godly men. The argument of the use of "sons of God" or *bene ha'Elohim* in the Old Testament is that Job 1 refers to angels, thus Genesis 6 refers to angels as well. Personally, I see no reason for Job 1 referring to angels. It may be the dead saints as described in the book of Revelation (e.g. the twenty four elders in Rev 5). In my limited knowledge, I know not of any biblical passage that depicts hordes of angels assembling before God, while there were many accounts in Revelation of dead saints doing so. Furthermore despite being fallen, it is too presumptuous that angels would then become sexual and be capable for having offspring with daughters of men in Genesis 6 against "kind after kind".

Even when fallen, the demons clearly maintain a hierarchy. As taught by the Lord Jesus Himself when accused of casting out demons in the name of Belzeebub, responded in Matthew 12:25-27 that Satan has a kingdom and it is "his kingdom".

Matthew 12:26 - And if Satan cast out Satan, he is divided against himself; how shall then his kingdom stand?

Every kingdom has a hierarchy. Even in Revelation 9:11-12, there is a leader of the smoke locusts of the bottomless pit called Abaddon or Apollyon. Many believe these locusts to be demons, and the leader to be a demon as well, although a careful reading of the passage does not refer them to demons, and the king of this horde is referred to as the "angel of bottomless pit" not devil/demon. Nonetheless, the issue is that if these beings are indeed demons, they do keep a hierarchy. If it is a good angel implementing judgement, it is not out of the ordinary.

It would also be timely to mention that this passage in Revelation 9 clearly teaches one thing, that even to harm non-believers, permission from God was necessary, even at the end times. The smoke locusts were not permitted to take lives or even hurt vegetation. This is a clear teaching furthering from the entire account of Job that the protection of God is not only restricted to special people of God, but also to the unbelievers and all creation.

One might recall that Legion also required the permission of Christ to possess even swine, which were regarded as unclean creatures by the Jews (Matthew 8:31).

The Scriptures clearly teach that the power of the Devil and his demons are severely limited. It is God Who Alone is supreme and sovereign. It is not an issue of Satan being an opposing force against God to fight their spiritual war on Earth for souls. There is no battle of good and evil. There was never a chance for God's will to be derailed; the supposed opposing forces are actually part of the pieces to fulfil God's plan.

On this, one would notice that exorcisms and demon possessions are not mentioned in the epistles to the churches and also not described in the book of Revelation. Even in the Old Testament, there are no records of demonic possessions and exorcism. Saul was not possessed though he was troubled by the spirit, neither was the Witch of Endor by the ghost of Samuel the Prophet-Judge, nor was Nebuchadnezzar in Daniel 4:33 technically possessed by an evil spirit.

The only records of demonic possessions and exorcisms were in the time of Christ and the apostles. And this was at the height of the God plan when the Word took on flesh to dwell among men, and the following establishment of the Church by the apostles. It is vain imagination when in exorcisms and spiritual healings, there are attempts to cast out demonic possessions today if there are indeed any. If there is no clear record of demonic possession even in the last days as recorded in Revelation, and if vegetation and pigs can only be harmed upon God's permission, there is no scriptural basis to believe that possessions still exist today at the cessation of special revelation, complete at the canonization of the complete Scriptures. The focus of biblical demonology should not be a fascination on the names and power of the Devil and demons, but rather at their defeat for the glory of God.

Romans 16:19. We are to be innocent of evil, but wise about what is good. By knowing what is good alone, and what is not good, we can avoid evil without knowing evil itself.

Let our sense not perceive what is not of God. Let our senses not be the teachers of evil and perverseness to my soul.

Instead

Let our senses be the windows of our soul to see the goodness of God, and be used as tools to learn and do the things that He has commanded.

The believer should not be spending any effort to attack the devil, or to spend time defending against him. Satan has misled many into thinking that we should spend our time findings ways to defend or even attack the devil. That is foolishness and has led to idolatry and superstition, in the sense that we go to God only because we fear the devil, inevitable giving importance to the defeated foe, and giving God second place in our hearts, breaking the commandment given in Deuteronomy 6:4-5.

Satan's age old trick is to always to get us to undermine God, forget God, or give God any position but the first and foremost in our hearts. It is not to rob us of our will. Even the entering into Judas by Satan in Luke 22:3 was not a possession in the sense that an exorcism was required, but more along the lines of Peter's temptation to Christ in Matthew 16:23.

The real solution to dealing with the devil, is rather to have God on the top most position in our hearts. And all things will fall in place.

Matthew 6:33 - But seek ye first the kingdom of God, and his righteousness; and all these things shall be added unto you.

In obedience to God, it is naturally easy to resist the devil.

James 4:7 - Submit yourselves therefore to God. Resist the devil, and he will flee from you.

From the scriptures, the worse Satan can do, even at the time before Christ, required the permission of God. He does not have power unless it is given by God. And the worst allowed by God, would not be physical endangerment as expected of demonic possession or demons masquerading as aliens for physical abductions.

Ephesians 6:12 - For we wrestle not against flesh and blood, but against principalities, against powers, against the rulers of the darkness of this world, against spiritual wickedness in high places.

If we are plagued by the devil (like Job or in Revelation 9), it is because we did not submit in obedience to God's commandments, or we have and are given the privilege to be tested under the consent of God as in Job and Paul (2 Corinthians 12:7-10). In which case, it is also for the glory of God, and also that we may know that His grace is sufficient for us.

Article 11: Singlehood, Marriage, Friendships

This is a follow up to "Another Practical Guide to the Logic, Philosophy, and Thoughts of Christianity" Section 1 – Article 1.

Once married, there must not be any inappropriate actions or emotions outside one's marriage, regardless of what one feels. The "change of heart" or "sexual incompatibility" excuses just do not hold water in any sense. It is the same for any crushes or attractions that do not have clear directive from God. There should be no action or feeding of them. Until there is clear definitive direction from God, there has to be self-control, involving management of these. This is precisely what self-control. The clear definitive direction has to be clear, and not one's own delusion of seeing what they want to see.

The major difficulty in erotic relationships is that it is difficult to tell pure good emotions from the sinful desires. How many in the world had already failed to differentiate lust from pure sacrificial love?

It is so easy to "put asunder what God had put together" through our own sinful desires and confusion that man really has no excuse. For the following, I will illustrate from some examples that I have known and seen around me.

One must first notice that the heart is vulnerable to confusion during loneliness. All too often, the very things that destroy marriages occur during periods of loneliness and helplessness. There is no lack of "Don Juan" libertines (both male and female) that had exploited the loneliness of the traveler in strange land; the lonely soul; the grieving soul recovering from loss of loved ones or reeling from heartbreak. Human hearts are vulnerable at these points. While God certainly does send human comforters, so does

Satan (if permitted by God) send in the destroyer of marriages. In this vulnerable state, one easily "falls in love" or develops such feelings. One can clearly see this in how people "fall in love" when travelling overseas, or find a replacement after a break-up or passing of spouse. It is the tendency of human nature to look for support. If one is not wary or guarded, they end up with the destroyer of their matrimony.

The other worldly snare would be the concept of platonic relationship and confidantes. Nowhere in the Bible can an example of close platonic relationship be found between opposite genders. Of course friendship between the two genders are there, and there certainly is nothing wrong with it. Did not our Lord Jesus have friendship with Mary Magdalene who became the first to see the resurrected Lord? Did not Paul mention Priscilla (Romans 16:3) as his fellow co-worker? Yet the problem is close confidantes in a platonic relationship, worse still outside marriage. No spouse should have a confidante outside marriage. The purpose of marriage is to be one. There is already no good outcome from the complaining spouse who brings the problem of the matrimony to outsider friends, much more for the complaining spouse to bring the problems of the matrimony to another of the opposite gender! While complaining to others out of the marriage of the same gender, it is already revealing the cracks of the marriage to outsiders/strangers/the prowling lion. When complaining to one of the opposite gender, is not the hidden message, "I'm not happy with my marriage, I want something else."?

Fools do this all too often under the guise of "confiding with friends". The foolishness and delusion of this confiding has been the cause of many broken marriages. How many quarrels have occurred from the unhappy spouse that his/her weaknesses are exposed by the other spouse to outsiders?

How many extra-marital affairs have started from confiding marriage problems to another outside of the other gender? I have in my short life seen an extramarital affair develop right under my nose when a male colleague with a troubled marriage started confiding his troubles with an unattached female colleague. Under the guise of pity, she would spend a lot of time to listen. Under the guise of sharing his trouble, he would spend more time with the girl. And within a couple of weeks, the extra-marital started. Oh the deceitfulness of the heart (Jeremiah 17:9)!

Is it not already taught in Jeremiah 9:4: "Take ye heed every one of his neighbour, and trust ye not in any brother: for every brother will utterly supplant, and every neighbour will walk with slanders."

Psalm 12:2: "They speak vanity everyone with his neighbour: with flattering lips and with a double heart do they speak."

It is modern day psychological garbage that people have to vent or somehow off load their problems or they will go mad. This has become the basis for confidantes outside marriage. Some even feel that they can turn to family members and spouses within the marriage. But do we forget who truly is trustworthy and has the power to help us? Is it not the Lord God Alone Who can be our true confidante and help (Psalm 20:7; Psalm 62:8; Psalm 121:2; Psalm 124:8)? What did the Lord Jesus do in Gethsemane in His hour of anguish? He prayed to the Father over confiding in His disciples who all fell asleep after professing that they would not deny Him but did it thrice (Matthew 26:30-47).

Did not Psalm 118:8 say clearly, "It is better to trust in the LORD than to put confidence in man."?

Micah 7:5-6 : Trust ye not in a friend, put ye not confidence in a guide: keep the doors of thy mouth from her that lieth in thy bosom. For the son dishonoureth the father, the daughter riseth up against her mother, the daughter in law against her mother in law; a man's enemies are the men of his own house.

Let us learn only to rely on the Lord Alone.

Article 12: Importance of Words – Part 1: Repent

When God says 'no', it is no. When He says 'yes', there is no hidden meaning or additional meaning. When He says six days, it is six days. We are not smart enough to double guess. And in most cases in the Bible, He does not speak for us to double guess.

Balaam asked. The answer was no. He asked again and again and he was permitted to his own condemnation.

God is not man to change His mind. He is immutable. The few occasions where the Bible recorded that God repented, as in the case of Noah's flood in Genesis 6:6 when God repented that He created man, it has to be read in context. In context, it is anthropomorphism, where we psychologically project ourselves. In some ways it is eisegesis (reading into Scripture) when we think it is possible for God to repent. An Eternal, All knowing God cannot repent. Because He knew beginning to end, otherwise we worship a limited being and he is not God because if He does not know all, His aseity is in question.

In context the passage means that God is showing man that man does NOT deserve to be created and He is wiping them out, with the exception of those He is gracious to. It is not God repenting and regretting per se, but He is showing that because man is unrepentant, He, even though He cannot regret and repent, repents to show man that they are not worthy. It is an act of final condescension before the flood to show the unrepentant evildoers that God is sufficiently upset at them to show that He cares, loves, and is merciful and gracious enough.

Let us consider why God should care to "repent"? Is it not in His power to simply abandon Earth to her devices? He can simply create another world in another six days or less, could He not? As David asked in the psalms very appropriately, "What is man?" that God should care (Psalm 8)? Job asked the same thing that what is he that God should bother if he sinned or not (Job 7:17)?

To fully understand the simple phrase of "God repented" requires wisdom from above. And it is perhaps not possible for a fool such as myself to explain it clearly in words as I am attempting to.

Yet, if any should have no less wisdom that this fool, let us at least hold on to the fact that it is not that God repented but rather that it is to say, man should repent but they did not. And He is all loving and gracious to care even for us to wipe us out to show us, in some sense of leading by example. And so for this purpose, we have in His Word to us, "repented" and it does mean what it means without question to His aseity and immutability.

This applies also to Exodus 32:14 and 1 Samuel 15:11 where God apparently "repented" or "regretted". Rather than that God repented and regretted, it is anthropomorphism and that He repented (in unimaginable love and mercy) because the culprits at hand, refused to.

Numbers 23:19 God is not a man, that he should lie; neither the son of man, that he should repent: hath he said, and shall he not do it? or hath he spoken, and shall he not make it good?

At first glance, it may appear that the verse contradicts all the verses on God's "repentance", yet this is a lack of clarity on God's nature. Rather, it is a clear affirmation of His aseity, love, and mercy that God has in all affairs of His dealings with His creation, even in their destruction. It is due to our failed repentance that He does.

Article 13: Importance of Words – Part 2: Heart speak

People cannot be trusted. They say one thing and do another. Some may claim they were forced to say something at a time or that they did not mean it later. Some may claim what they say did not reflect their thoughts.

Man's words deserve little trust. And words need not be spoken words. It can be thoughts.

I have heard many Christians claim that simply thinking about something bad is not a sin if it is without expression or action. However, a careful reading of Psalm 14:1 clearly teaches against such nonsensical imaginations. It is not acceptable to even think, wit h or without saying. It is preposterous for a justification to arise along the lines of "thinking is not as sin!".

Remember, the people in the days of Noah were judged based on their hearts.

Genesis 6:5 And GOD saw that the wickedness of man *was* great in the earth, and *that* every imagination of the thoughts of his heart *was* only evil continually.

To further illustrate the point that thoughts are just as important.

Psalm 14:1 - The fool hath said in his heart, There is no God. They are corrupt, they have done abominable works, there is none that doeth good.

The fool *said* in his heart. Not necessarily with the tongue. And so here it is.

But the Word of God, every word of it, must be treated and read carefully. For example the verse of Psalm 14:1 uses the word "said" - Strong's Concordance H559 אמר 'âmar aw-mar' . It is clearly "said" and not "thinks" as one would expect for the heart. For certainly the heart does not "speak".

We need to respect the word of God is important and read it as it is. Too often have we excused ourselves by trying to read into the word of God. God is not man to use/preserve wrong words for our carnal and foolish purposes. Every word must be taken seriously, otherwise meanings change. Sure it is a translation, but translators, especially KJV for English, had made great effort and respect to the word of God, with the understanding given by the Spirit.

Job 32:8 - But there is a spirit in man: and the inspiration of the Almighty giveth them understanding.

If we be children of God, let our words, whether in our hearts or verbalized be what they are.

Matthew 5:37 - But let your communication be, Yea, yea; Nay, nay: for whatsoever is more than these cometh of evil.

And if we be born again sons of God (Romans 8:14 - For as many as are led by the Spirit of God, they are the sons of God.), let us watch our speech too, whether it be by tongue or in the heart.

Article 14: "Into the Woods"

I deliberated over the writing of this article, as it may appear to some that I have committed the heinous act of eisegesis. Please note that I am by no means reading the film into the Word of God, but rather, I am showing how the film/musical can illustrate our desperate state in the light of the Word of the God. There are other articles in my other books that uses such illustration methods, particular in "Another Guide to the Logic, Philosophy and Thoughts of Christianity".

The 2014 film "Into the Woods" is from a shortened version of a complicated musical story line about famous characters from the Grimm Brothers stories (see https://en.wikipedia.org/wiki/Into_the_Woods_(film))

The film teaches a moral that the "wants" and desires of the characters did not leave them happily ever after, and that every action has a consequence, no matter how small.

While the film has clear illustrations to the consequences of our moral choices, one song - "Last Midnight" stood out clearly to illustrate the Original Sin, and the pain and problems of modern humanistic ideas.

When Eve was first tempted, it was a temptation to depart from the guidance of God. She wanted to be independent to determine right and wrong and be like God. Aside from the lust of the eyes, of the flesh and lust of the mind, she wanted autonomy. She wanted to be able to determine right and wrong.

The humanistic ideas embedded in Neo-Darwinism of today is a direct attempt to remove ideas of God and give man the ability the right to say what is right and what is wrong. We hear the echo of "Who decides what is right and wrong? Why must I conform to society?" in the post modernistic ideas of today.

This is a direct consequence of the Original Sin. When man "knows good and evil", they decide their own good and evil, and conflict ensues. They forgot that it is God Who decides what is right and wrong. Man can never do it properly because of his ignorance and lack of omniscience. The lack of knowledge of everything cannot allow one to determine right and wrong correctly. With differing skills, differing knowledge, man can never agree within mankind what is right and wrong. A language novice will say some half-baked phrasing is right and this will be disagreed upon by an expert. Life in the fallen world will move on in turmoil, groaning in pain from the result of these ignorance and improper discernment. Each man gives in to what they want, as exactly depicted by the "Last Midnight" song.

Illustrated in the song is the pursuit of blame. No one cares what is right and wrong, but rather who to blame. All the characters are at fault or have contributed to dire consequences, yet they were only concerned with pushing the blame as in the song "Your fault" in the film/play.

Was that not exactly what happened when Adam, Eve, and the snake stood before God?

Adam blamed God for giving him Eve, who was the source of sin.

Eve blamed the snake for deceiving her.

The snake was the wisest to not shift the blame. Surely, in my fallen mind, we can surely suggest that it is God's fault for creating the snake and/or putting the tree right there in the Garden within reach. Why even give them the chance to be tempted? In fact, Adam did allude to blaming God when he blamed Eve, whom God had put next to him.

The snake/Satan did better than Man. Far better. And is clearly much wiser than Man.

Neither Adam nor Eve cared or acknowledged what they did was wrong. Like the Witch's song "Last Midnight", they were only concerned about who to blame.

And here, to an relatively insightful part of the lyrics of the song

"You're so nice
You're not good
You're not bad
You're just nice"

There are clear humanistic ideas at play. The Word of God clearly tells us that we are rotten to the core. Calvin's "Total Depravity of Man" sums up the doctrine of man's hopelessness.

Humanism expects Man to just be "nice". Since everyone has differing views of good and evil, let us all be nice so we can get along. To the humanist, being nice is being good. And being good is to be nice and tolerant. Since no one knows and can decide what is right and wrong, let us just accept everything and everyone and whatever they do. That would make one nice. Forget what's right.

And as the Witch in the film sang,

"I'm not good
I'm not nice
I'm just right".

There is a slight convoluted meaning here, where the "not good" refers to the world's view of good, rather than what is good. Without discussing the character's motive and proposed action in the film/musical to sacrifice Jack to save everyone, it is in my opinion arguable that objective good is the same as what is right. But the meaning of good had been perverted in today's worldview to become so subjective that it now has little objective meaning. Even being right, makes "right" imply a pure logical and greater good effect. Yet that is not so. "Right" is correct, and correctness is determined by God. So the lack of concern of right and wrong, or good and evil, are in fact synonymous and yet also separate. One can do the right thing to result in evil, and one can do the wrong thing that can result in good (e.g. Joseph's brothers selling him, the crucifixion of Christ). God is beyond all these good and evil or right and wrong concepts, thus He Alone can determine them.

In a sense, the Witch's frustration in the song may reflect that of the jaded Christian, weary and worn down by the world. It is suggestive of the voice of the few that cares about "right and wrong". Frustrated with the foolishness, the witch decides to leave the characters to deal with their own plight and the consequences of their own actions i.e. their choice to be "nice". She acknowledges she is just the hitch that no one believes and everyone else as "the world".

"I'm a hitch
I'm what no one believes
I'm the witch
You're all liars and thieves
Like his father
Like his son will be, too
Oh, why bother?
You'll just do what you do"

The Witch knows exactly that they will just do what they do. And that is precisely what Man will do until they are illuminated and saved by God. Unless redeemed by God, there is no doubt that each and every one will just keep doing what we feel is right.

Judges 21:25 In those days there was no king in Israel: every man did that which was right in his own eyes.

As the Witch gave up singing.

"I'm leaving you alone
You can tend the garden, it's yours
Separate and alone
Everybody down on all fours"

Many a Christian is also tempted to do the same to walk away and ask, "Why bother?"

Matthew 10:14: And whosoever shall not receive you, nor hear your words, when ye depart out of that house or city, shake off the dust of your feet.

We do ask that. But God did not. In fact, God's immeasurable patience has held out since the time of Noah's Ark till today and will do so until the last days which is not too far. At that moment, woe be upon all of creation except for the redeemed.

1 Peter 4:17 - For the time is come that judgment must begin at the house of God: and if it first begin at us, what shall the end be of them that obey not the gospel of God?

Let us now recognize our own faults and not push the blame. Let us be swift to bow and humble ourselves before the Lord in repentance. Let us not be like the characters in the film, and buy into humanistic ideas of "being nice". We must care for being good and being right. Not the "good" and "right" determined by our own ignorance, but by the very Word of God.

www.ingramcontent.com/pod-product-compliance
Lightning Source LLC
Chambersburg PA
CBHW081636040426
42449CB00014B/3340